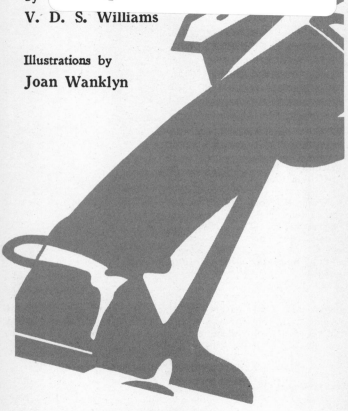

R

by

V. D. S. Williams

Illustrations by
Joan Wanklyn

Published for
THE BRITISH HORSE SOCIETY

Published in 1977 by
BARRON'S EDUCATIONAL SERIES, INC.
Woodbury, New York • London • Toronto

First Edition 1954
Second Edition 1964
Third Edition 1966

Published in 1977 by
Barron's Educational Series, Inc.
113 Crossways Park Drive
Woodbury, New York 11797

© EP Publishing Ltd. 1970

Library of Congress Catalog Card No. 76-54799

Library of Congress Cataloging in Publication Data
Williams, Lilian Brenda, 1895-
  Riding.
  1. Horsemanship.   I. Title.
SF309.W55   1976   798'.23   76-54799
ISBN 0-8120-0732-8

International Standard Book No. 0-8120-0732-8

PRINTED IN THE UNITED STATES OF AMERICA

2345   045   98765432

To my husband whose guidance and example have been an inspiration to me and to whom I owe everything

FOREWORD

Throughout the ages many Britons have found enjoyment with horses. How strange it is that in this age of mechanisation and craze for speed there are more people riding than ever before.

Whatever the pastime, whether it be fishing, cricket or even hiking, perhaps the greatest change is that the fisherman, cricketer or hiker has realized that the more he or she knows about a pastime the greater will be his or her enjoyment. We have, I fear, to pay for our sports, and by being efficient we will get more value for our money.

Mrs. Williams is a great horsewoman; she has studied the art of horsemanship and has certainly proved that this study was worthwhile. There are some who may know as much as Mrs. Williams, but there are few who have been so ready to pass on their great knowledge to others and so increase their enjoyment.

This book, so full of information and brilliantly illustrated by Miss Wanklyn, should be read and re-read by every rider, for it is certain that he or she will derive greater pleasure from knowing more about how to ride. It is full of information which has taken the expert many years to learn. Have it by your bedside and I am confident that every one of you will gain from knowing more about how to ride and care for the horse.

We depend upon the horse for our pleasure and this we will only get in full if a happy understanding and sympathy exist between horse and rider. The rider must know how to look after his or her horse, and must know how to fit the saddlery and care for the animal which is his or her companion. In instances where the pronouns *he* and *him* appear, they have been used to avoid awkward prose. It should be understood that these references apply to all riders, whether male or female.

Colonel and Mrs. Williams have done much for us all, but I do not believe they have ever done more than by producing this book.

M. P. Ansell

Chairman, British Horse Society.

CONTENTS

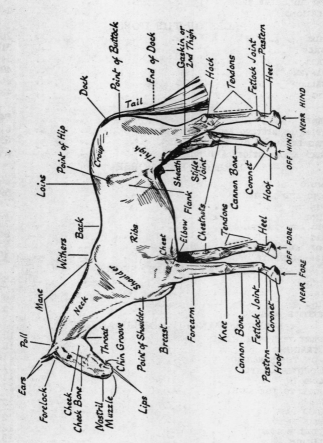

The points of a horse.

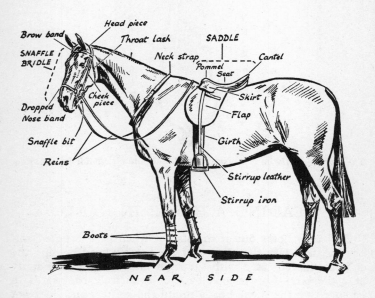

Brow band
Head piece
Throat lash
SNAFFLE
BRIDLE
Neck strap
SADDLE
Cantel
Pommel
Seat
Cheek
piece
Skirt
Dropped
Nose band
Flap
Snaffle bit
Girth
Reins
Stirrup leather
Stirrup iron
Boots

NEAR SIDE

A horse saddled for riding.

FIRST PRINCIPLES

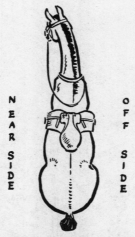

The near-side of the horse is always the left side, and the off-side its right side.

LEADING A HORSE IN HAND

To lead a horse out of the stables when he is saddled and bridled, first take the reins over the horse's head holding the ends in the left hand with the right hand on the reins fairly near the bit. Always look back or even walk backwards to be sure that the horse bends round the corners and does not hurt himself.

If the passage out of the stables is narrow or the turns sharp, take great care not to bump the horse's hip on a sharp corner by turning too quickly and not looking where the horse is going. The horse may be seriously damaged through knocking the hip joint and injuring it.

Always look backwards when leading a horse out.

Be careful not to knock the horse's hip when coming through a doorway.

How to mount.

MOUNTING AND DISMOUNTING

Mounting

Before mounting see that the girths are tight.

(1) Stand level with the horse's shoulder on the near side, facing the horse's tail. Take the reins and stick in the left hand. Grasp the horse's neck or mane just in front of the withers, take hold of the stirrup leather with the right hand and place the left foot well home in the stirrup, toe pointing downwards so as not to dig the horse in the side. (2) Take hold of the saddle with the right hand and (3) spring lightly up, straighten the left knee, pass the right leg over the horse's back, being careful not to touch him. Allow the body to sink gently into the saddle without a bump, placing the right foot in the stirrup without looking down.

Dismounting

The safest way to dismount is as follows :—

Kick both feet out of the stirrups. (1) Place the left hand, with the stick, on the horse's neck, and the right hand on the pommel of the saddle with fingers pointing down. (2) Take the weight of the body on the hands and lightly vault off, landing on the toes as in a jump, with knees bent.

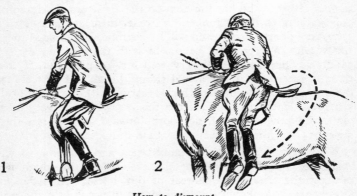

1   2

How to dismount.

The correct seat.

THE SEAT

A large divergence will be found in how different people
sit on a saddle. If a rider has been taught to jump at an early
stage and before he has understood the elementary principles
appertaining to the training of a horse, in most cases he will
have very short stirrups and will be leaning well forward, most
likely with a rounded back and with the seat out of the
saddle. This may be all very well for jumping, but, if the
rider is interested in the art of riding, he should first study
the ordinary balanced seat which must go with the training of
a horse. Having once mastered this, it will be a very easy
matter for him to get a little more forward and shorten his
stirrups; the jumping seat will come quite easily.

We will now study the balanced seat and in doing so we
shall discover that it will be the easiest way in which we
can get the maximum control of our horse. In order to
attain this the rider must sit well down in the saddle and not

Stirrups too short.

Stirrups too long.

just rest on top of it. The stirrup leathers should be of such a length as to be comfortable. A rough guide is that, when the rider's legs are stretched down, the tread of the irons should come just below the ankle joint. If the leathers are too long, the rider will always be groping for them; consequently, his toes will go down, his legs will go forward, he will lose his balance, and he will have to resort to the reins in order to hold himself in the saddle. If they are too short, he will lean too far forward in order to keep his balance, his legs will go back with the toes pointing down, and it will thus become impossible for him to give the correct indications, known as aids, to the horse.

The head must be erect, free and unconstrained. If it is thrust forward or kept in a stiff position the rider will become stiff throughout his body which will immediately react on the horse and cause him to resist. The body should be upright and supple, the shoulders thrown back and they should be kept parallel to the horse's shoulders. The strongest aid comes from the back. If the back is allowed to sag or be loose, it cannot give an aid because it is not in a position to do so. By tucking his seat underneath him, the rider only succeeds in throwing his weight back on the horse's loins and unbalancing himself. But, if he braces his back and pushes down with a strong forward inclination as if all the drive were going out through his knees, he can then produce, together with the legs, a tremendously strong aid and in this way gain most control over his horse. He can produce impulsion or, conversely, a smooth reduction of pace in this manner, but its great importance lies in the fact that it is this back-aid which produces the activity in the horse's hind-legs and, therefore, the motive power. It can now be seen how important it is for the rider's back to be straight and supple. It must never be rounded or stiff.

Back too round.   *Body too stiff.*

The legs should be stretched well down, the thighs flat, the knees close to the flaps of the saddle and the toes kept in a natural position to the front so that the horse may feel the legs while not being touched with the spurs. The heels should be pressed down lower than the toes. The lower leg must be at such an angle as always to keep the stirrup leathers perpendicular to the ground. This leg position is very important because it is through the legs that the aids are given, therefore, it is imperative that they should always be in a position to give the aid at a precise moment. If the legs are carried too far forward, or too far backward, they are not in a suitable position, and the aid will come a fraction late. The rider will first have to correct his position before he can apply the aid; consequently, the psychological moment has passed, and the rider has missed his chance of giving a directive or a possible correction.

It has been said that the rider must sit well down in the saddle. This is also of great importance, because it is through his seat that he can feel an evasion or a resistance from his horse. If his seat is continually bumping up and down in the saddle there will be moments, when the seat is off the saddle, that he cannot feel what the horse is doing and so he could miss an opportunity of administering a reprimand or anticipating an evasion. It is now easy to see why the rider should sit deep down in the saddle and, except in the rising trot, his seat should not leave the saddle.

It is not necessary for the rider to grip continually with his knees as this would tend to make him draw them up in the saddle; then the toes would go down, the position of the legs lost, and he would be gripping with the calves of his legs. If the heels and knees are pushed well down with the knees turned on to the saddle so that the toes are pointing in a natural position, it will not be difficult for the rider to keep his balance with a minimum contact. But, if the toes are pointing out, the rider would, quite unconsciously, be touching his horse with his spurs when not even intending to give an aid. This, naturally, would cause great confusion in the mind of the horse and not a little irritation.

The rider's ankles and knees should be supple, as if they were springs capable of taking his weight when required, and at no time should they be stiff. Only one-third of the foot, the ball, should be placed in the stirrup. If the foot is "home" the ankle will lose its elasticity. The feet are occasionally pressed "home" in the stirrups in cross-country riding.

The arms should hang naturally down to the elbows which should be lightly touching the sides. The forearm should be in a straight line through the reins to the horse's mouth. The hands, with the thumbs uppermost, should be kept still but they must be soft and supple with the wrists slightly rounded, held above the pommel of the saddle and roughly 3 inches apart.

It will be found that this seat will be of the utmost value to the rider. With it he can get maximum control of his horse because he can be ready instantaneously to apply any aid at any moment. He will, in fact, be one with his horse.

HANDS

It is essential for a rider to have good hands so let us consider what is meant by good hands.

Through the reins, and therefore the hands, the rider has his fingers on, one might say, the pulse of the horse; he regulates the pace, directs the horse, and asks "flexions" through this medium and it is of the utmost importance that he understands the influences he produces in this manner. The hands at all times must be light and responsive. They must be able to "give" and to "take" instantaneously, so much so that it becomes almost a reflex action.

Later it will be shown how the whole of a horse's training revolves round his mouth. In order to produce a beautiful looking and well balanced animal it is necessary for the horse to accept and hold the bit lightly in his mouth and to keep an even contact with both reins. He will then be ready at the slightest indication of the rider to obey any command given him. None of this can be accomplished unless the rider has light and delicate hands so that he is capable of feeling and correcting the slightest resistance on the part of the horse. If the horse resists in his mouth it is felt throughout his body which becomes stiff and unyielding.

The rider does not use his hands alone; they must always work in conjunction with his legs and back. But it is the sense of touch through the fingers that makes or mars a horse's mouth, and the whole future of a rider's success in riding and training horses will depend upon whether his hands are sensitive to every reaction on the horse's mouth. He must know when and how his hands should act and when they should be soft. They should remain at the same level and be still. When acting they must not be drawn back but used as in the "squeezing-of-a-sponge" and then remain soft and still again when the horse has given to the demanded flexion and be ready to come into immediate action once more at the slightest sign of resistance.

The hands must remain at the same height, one on each side of the horse's withers and just above them. On no account should they cross over to the opposite side. If either rein crossed the withers, that rein, coming in contact with the horse's neck, would throw the weight onto the opposite shoulder thus defeating its object.

The rider's upper arms should hang loosely, close to his sides, but they must not be clamped there with a consequent stiff fore-arm, for in this way it would be impossible for him to keep his hands still. The fore-arms and wrists must be supple and loose so that they can act as a sort of buffer between the movement of the rider's body and the horse's mouth. As the rider becomes more efficient he will sit more erect and still so the horse will feel no movement whatever when the hands are being polite and soft.

A very common fault seen in riding is too much movement of the hands. A horse's mouth is very sensitive and it is the rider's aim that it should remain so. But, if the hands are continually working backwards and forwards with every movement of his body, it is not surprising that the horse's mouth becomes insensitive, because he gets a continual aid with every step he takes, and this confuses him.

It will now be seen how important it is for the rider to have a strong and independent seat because he must never use the reins in order to maintain his position in the saddle. The reins are only meant to guide and direct the movements of the horse and the rider must remember that the softer the hands the softer will be the horse, whilst heavy hands can only produce a heavy horse.

HOW TO HOLD THE REINS

How to hold the reins of a snaffle bridle in one hand.

Snaffle Bridle—reins in one hand

If the rider wishes to put the reins in one hand, he transfers the rein from the right hand into the left hand so that it passes across the palm of the hand and rests on top of the left rein.

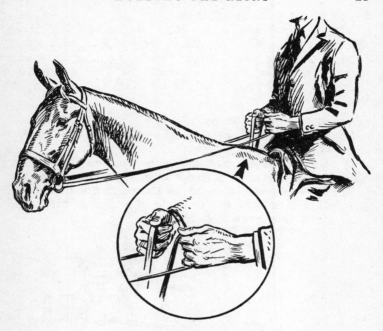

How to hold the reins of a snaffle bridle.

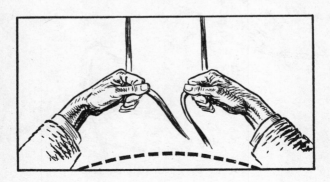

Snaffle Bridle—reins in both hands

The left rein should be held in the left hand passing below the fourth finger with the slack of the rein going across the palm of the hand, and between the first finger and thumb. Alternatively it can be held between the third and fourth fingers. The right rein is held in the same way in the right hand.

How not to hold the Reins

(a) The hands must not be held straight with the thumbs uppermost.

(b) They should not be flat with the knuckles on top. In both these cases the hands would lose their elasticity.

(c) The wrists should not be unduly rounded as this would make them stiff and it would also tend to force the elbows out away from the body.

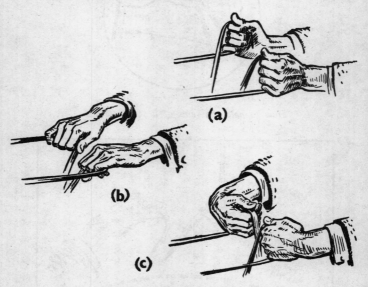

Incorrect ways of holding the reins

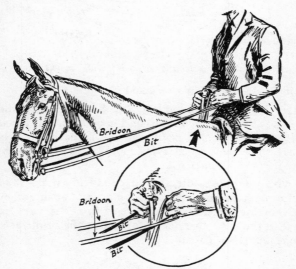

How to hold the reins of a double bridle

Double Bridle—reins in both hands

When a double bridle is used, the little finger of each hand should divide the reins, with the bridoon reins held on the outside.

The importance of holding the bridoon reins on the outside can be understood when it is pointed out that all schooling work should be done with a snaffle bridle. With it the rider positions and directs his horse (always in conjunction with the legs). Thus, with the bridoon reins held on the outside the rider has more definite control than with those held on the inside. The double bridle adds elegance to the horse and gives the rider more control.

How to hold the reins of a double bridle in one hand.

Double Bridle—reins in one hand

Place the little finger of the left hand between the two left reins with the bridoon rein on the outside, and the second finger between the two right reins with the bridoon on the outside. The slack of the reins should pass between the first finger and the thumb (a).

If, with a double bridle, the rider suddenly wants to put the reins in one hand to catch a swinging gate, or in some other emergency, he can transfer both reins from the right hand to the left in the same manner as for the snaffle bridle as shown on page 20, also (b) above.

FIRST LESSONS

In the first lessons the pupil should be put on a very quiet horse with the instructor leading him on a lunge rein. At the walk he should be made to stand up in his stirrups and then sit down and this must be repeated until he gets some idea of balance, when the instructor could let the horse trot gently whilst running along beside him. At the trot the pupil must try to allow the horse to throw him up and, if he then attempts to help this movement by rising at the same time, he will find himself in the air when one diagonal comes to the ground, whilst he comes down in the saddle and sits when the other diagonal comes to the ground. If this exercise is continually repeated the rider will soon find that he is rising and sitting with the greatest of ease.

But this movement can easily be exaggerated and the rider must try not to rise from the stirrups with stiff knees because,

The instructor leading the horse.

if he does, he will find his body becoming stiff and he will be inclined to rise in front of the movement of the horse, which is most unsightly and unbalanced.

It is as well to have a neck-strap which the pupil can hold, as it gives great confidence and it also helps him to keep in the saddle without disturbing the horse's mouth, but it is better for the pupil to look upon it as an emergency and only use it when in danger of losing his balance.

On the Lunge

Lunge work is an excellent way of getting the rider down in the saddle and of giving him a strong and independent seat.

A pupil on the lunge

It also enables him to concentrate on his seat without having to worry about his horse. The instructor has the lunge rein fastened at one end to the cavesson which is placed on the horse's head on top of the bridle. He holds the other end in his hand and the horse is made to go round him in a large circle by the aid of his voice and a long whip. Side reins are fitted at one end to the girths, not lower than the rider's knees, and fastened to the bit at the other end. They should be of such length as to allow the horse's head to be in front of the perpendicular so as not to restrict his paces. It is important for the horse to be obedient and quiet because the rider will be doing this work first without reins and then without both reins and stirrups. At first he walks and, when the rider has got his confidence, the horse is allowed to trot and finally to canter.

This work must be practised for some time and when the pupil is beginning to understand the rhythm of the horse, has found his balance and has confidence at all paces, then is the time for his stirrups to be taken away.

He should now be able to sit deep in the saddle with his legs stretched down as far as possible, elbows to his sides,

head erect and arms either folded or lightly resting on his thighs. He must be supple, upright, yet loose everywhere. Only the ankles are flexed so as to prevent the toes from pointing downwards. He should not grip but remain in the saddle by balance alone.

There are many different exercises which can be performed on the lunge to supple the rider and strengthen his seat.

1. Arms swinging alternately—first one and then the other —at the trot.
2. Leaning down and touching the toe—first with one hand and then with the other at—the trot.
3. Pivoting the trunk round in rhythm with the canter.

PACES OF THE HORSE
THE AIDS

The horse in nature roams about at will and moves or not as inclination dictates. When he is mounted and ridden by man he has to learn to lose his own personality and submerge his wishes to those of his master. Being a dumb animal he cannot be told in so many words what to do. How, then, is this to be achieved?

Through the centuries the horse has been the friend and willing servant of man, and this method of understanding a horse has been handed down to us through the centuries from the time of Xenophon, the great Greek warrior who lived in 400 B.C.

The aids are the means whereby the rider conveys his instruction to his horse and which the horse must learn to obey implicitly with willingness and grace. Naturally some horses begin to understand what is required of them much quicker than others. Some are willing learners, others resent another personality impressing his will upon them. The rider must never force a horse into a certain position as it would impair his action, produce a resistance, and the position will be lost the moment the reins are relaxed. The aids must be used with perseverance and repetition until the horse knows exactly what is required of him and immediately obeys.

There are two kinds of aids, natural and artificial.

Natural Aids

(1) *The Hands* give direction to the horse and regulate the energy created by the legs and body. The rider's hands should always be very light, sensitive and responsive. They must be capable of acting or giving instantaneously. Except when the horse is walking relaxed on a loose rein, there should always be a light contact with the horse's mouth. Sometimes it need only be with one rein (the one on the soft side of the horse) whilst the other rein gives, but a light

contact should be maintained at all times. This is important because the rider cannot give with one rein unless there is a contact with the other, otherwise there is no meaning to the aid and nothing would be gained.

(2) *The Legs* create impulsion and control the hindquarters. It is most important for the legs to work always in conjunction with the hands. Thus, if the rider asks for a flexion with the right rein, the right leg must act *at the same time* to demand that flexion and the moment the horse responds the rider must sit very quiet until he wishes to give another order. The legs can act at the girths or just behind them, according to the movement the rider wishes to execute. They should be kept still and close to the horse's sides ready to come into action at a moment's notice. The horse must learn to obey immediately the lightest action of the rider's legs. He must go forward at the slightest touch and likewise walk, trot, canter, turn, reduce or increase pace or halt when commanded.

(3) *The Body* can create impulsion, reduce or increase the pace and cause the horse to change direction. Here again the body must work in conjunction with the legs and hands. The rider's back, when sitting correctly, can be the cause of the strongest aid the rider can produce. If the back is straight, when it is braced it can help the legs produce more extension or, conversely, it can help to reduce the pace according to how much the hands allow or resist the impulsion created. Its great value is that it creates impulsion by causing the horse to lower his haunches thus getting his hind-legs more under him when he is in a better position to go forward or to come back at the rider's will. Also, by shifting the weight to one side or the other, the rider's body helps in making the horse turn or go sideways on two tracks.

(4) *The Voice* can assist in controlling the horse in the early stages of his training. Before a horse is backed when on the lunge he soon gets used to the trainer's voice and, if a different tone is used for the walk, trot and canter, the horse will soon learn to answer to the voice alone. When the time comes to mount the horse, the voice will be found a great help in

teaching him the rein and leg aids, and it can be dropped as soon as he understands.

Artificial Aids

(1) *The Whip* can be used to reinforce the leg aids on a sluggish horse in order to help create impulsion. It is better to use a light cutting whip (a hazel cut from a bush makes a very good one) to keep the horse going-on rather than to use the legs too much, as he would soon get callous to the continual movement of the legs and would then not obey the aids given. It should be used behind the girths with just a light tap as a reminder to answer the rider's leg aids.

(2) *The Spurs* can be used in conjunction with the legs to create quicker obedience, but they should be used sparingly. It is better not to use spurs with a young horse. He should get to know and answer the leg aids without them. As he gets to understand the different aids given by the rider and obeys them promptly, spurs can be worn. They give elegance to the rider and can be used if necessary. Spurs should not be worn by a rider until he is sure he can use them when he wishes and not apply them each time a leg aid is given.

(3) *The Martingale* is not an aid to use when training a horse. It is a mistake to hold a horse's head down by force because, directly the martingale is taken away, the head will go up again. In fact some horses who are used to wearing a tight standing martingale like to hold their heads against this strap and if it were removed the rider would be in danger of getting a blow in the face. The horse should be asked to put his head down with the rein and leg aid acting on the side to which the horse resists and when he has learnt this lesson it will be found that he will keep it there. A martingale is useful on a young horse who will fling up his head and then bolt. In this case it should be fitted just long enough to stop the head from going too high and so that he does not feel it when the head is carried correctly. A standing mar tingale is the better one to use in this case; the reason for this will be seen later in this book.

THE WALK

The Aids. Unless otherwise stated, the rider should always sit as described under the heading of the Seat. In order to make the horse walk forward he must close both legs, brace the muscles of his seat and back and ease the reins. As soon as the horse advances at the required pace, the rider must sit quiet with long reins and the lightest of contacts with the horse's mouth.

On turning a corner the rider should bend the horse to the direction in which he wishes to go, *i.e.*, in going round a corner to the right the rider turns the horse's head slightly to the right with the right rein. This should be supported by the left rein which allows the degree of bend. The right leg acting at the girths, keeps up the impulsion and prevents the horse from falling in, and the left leg, acting behind the girths, prevents the horse from throwing his quarters to the left. The rider must take care not to bring his left hand across the horse's neck in order to make him turn by the use of the indirect rein, because this would put more weight on this rein and on to his right shoulder which would un-balance him and make him lose his rhythm. This principle applies throughout.

To come back from a walk to a halt, the rider braces his seat and back muscles in a pushing down movement as if the impulsion is coming out through his knees and, by asking with the hand on the stiff side and resisting with the other hand, the horse will come to a halt (see page 104 for hard side). The horse should stand with his weight evenly distributed on all four legs.

Bracing the seat and back to reduce pace

The sequence of steps at the walk.

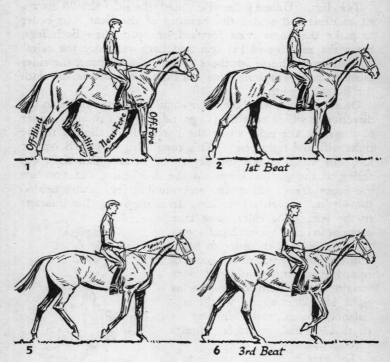

The walk is a pace of 4 time. A horse will lift each leg up and put it down again separately, and, as all impulsion should come from behind, he should commence walking with a hind-leg thus : (1) near-hind ; (2) near-fore ; (3) off-hind ; (4) off-fore. If a handkerchief is tied round the horse's near-hind and the instructor leads him forward slowly saying : 1, 2, 3, 4 as each foot comes to the ground, the sequence of legs can be well demonstrated.

The sequence of steps at the walk.

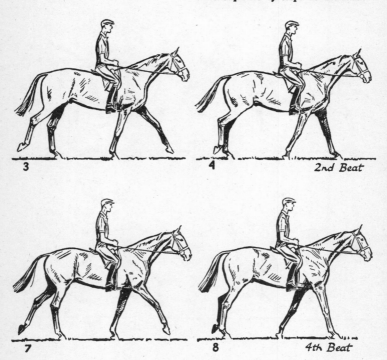

In these illustrations it can be seen that the horse commences with his near-hind which in No. 1 is just about to come to the ground which it does in No. 2 making the first beat. In Nos. 1, 2 and 3 the near-fore moves forward to take the weight in No. 4 making the second beat, whilst the off-hind in No. 3 is off the ground, is being brought forward in Nos. 4 and 5 and, in No. 6, takes the weight and makes the third beat. Finally the off-fore starts going forward in No. 5, finishes with the fourth beat in No. 8 and the cycle starts all over **again**.

The sequence of steps at the trot.

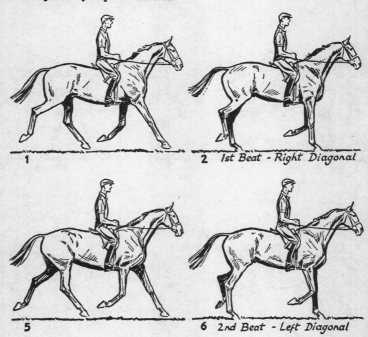

1

2   *1st Beat - Right Diagonal*

5

6   *2nd Beat - Left Diagonal*

THE TROT

The trot is a pace of 2 time. The horse springing alternately from one pair of diagonals to the other. Illustration
No. 1 shows the moment of suspension with all four feet off
the ground. In No. 2 the off-fore and near-hind (right
diagonal) are taking the weight for the first beat, whilst the
near-fore and off-hind (left diagonal) are coming forward in
Nos. 3, 4 and 5, to take the weight in No. 6 (second beat),
when it will be seen that the right diagonal has already left
the ground, is being carried forward in Nos. 7 and 8, and

The sequence of steps at the trot.

through the moment of suspension (No. 1) to commence taking the weight again in No. 2.

There are two methods which can be adopted at the trot: (1) the sitting, (2) the rising trot. The sitting trot is when the rider sits in the saddle and does not rise. He must remain very still and erect and his seat should not come off the saddle. This method will be found very tiring for the rider until he becomes efficient in the saddle as, until he has learnt to follow the movements of the horse, he will be bounced about and lose his balance. The sitting trot should not be employed with young horses until their back muscles are developed, nor in older horses just up from grass or when they have been out of work for some time. It is important for the horse's back to get strong before the rider sits for long periods. These back muscles are most important to the training of a horse and get strong and supple only if the horse is made to trot with a correct carriage and in rhythm.

If the rider sits too much before these back muscles are strong he will be in danger of making the horse dip his back to evade an unpleasant feeling. If this happens the rider will be in a lot of trouble as, instead of responding to a back aid by lowering his quarters and activating his hind legs producing forward impulsion, he will dip his back which acts on the hind quarters in the opposite way by heightening them and leaving his hind legs sprawling behind which shows itself in loss of rhythm and impulsion. Experienced riders will employ the sitting trot as the training progresses as in this way it is easier to produce and maintain a rhythmic trot full of impulsion.

The body is slightly forward in the rising trot.

In the rising trot, the rider sits in the saddle when one diagonal comes to the ground and, as the horse is propelled forwards, the rider allows himself to be thrust upwards, remaining out of the saddle with his weight on his knees and stirrups, while the other diagonal strikes the ground. In this trot the rider's body can be very slightly forward. He can trot on either the right or the left diagonal. He is said to be on the right diagonal when he comes down in the saddle as the horse's right diagonal comes to the ground and vice versa. He can soon find out which diagonal he is on by saying down to himself

as soon as he comes down in the
saddle and by noticing which fore-
leg comes to the ground as he says
it. The rider should practise
changing the diagonals, which he
can do by bumping the saddle for
one or three strides. If he does not
change and rides continually on the
same diagonal his horse will become very stiff and difficult to ride
on the neglected diagonal. The
rider will soon appreciate this
when he commences to train his
own horse.

Leaning too far forward.

The rider must not lean back
with his legs poking forward as in
this way he is inclined to lose his
balance and he will not be able to
apply his leg and back aids. Nor
should he lean forward as if he
were trying to pull the horse along
as this gets him in front of the

Leaning too far back.

movement and again he will be unable to apply the correct aids.

The Aids to Trot

The rider closes both legs on the horse and, by bracing the
muscles of his seat and back and easing both reins slightly,
he urges the horse forward into a trot. As soon as he advances
at the required pace, the rider must sit quiet and still, maintaining a light contact on the reins. If the horse reduces pace
before he is asked to, he must be urged on again in the same
way. To reduce the pace to a walk the rider applies the same
aids as in going from a walk to a halt.

Halting from the Trot

To reduce the pace from a trot to a halt, the rider uses
much stronger back and leg-aids than he does to go from a
walk to a halt, and, by resisting with one hand and

Reducing from a trot to a halt.

asking with the rein on the stiff side, it will be found that the horse will lower his haunches as seen in illustrations Nos. 2 and 3, and will come to a halt standing equally on all four legs as in No. 4

This is a very important exercise and should be practised continually because it is this aid that is going to be used throughout the training of a horse.   It is this back and leg-aid which drives the horse's hind-legs under him and can either reduce the pace or create impulsion at the wish of the rider. It is also of importance to make the horse stand correctly (No. 4 above) with his weight equally balanced on all four

The effect on the horse when the rider pulls him back by the reins and does

Reducing from a trot to a halt.

3   4

legs and not with one leg or the other stretched either forwards or backwards and he must remain on the bit.

The rider should take care not to pull the horse back with the hands alone.   If he does, the horse will throw up his head and hollow his back, thus leaving his hind-legs behind him and halting in a bad position.   This is well depicted in illustrations 2, 3 and 4 below, which shows the reaction of the horse to the rider leaning back with strong hands held high. He throws his weight on to his shoulders (No. 2) by raising his quarters and dipping his back as he comes to a halt with the hind legs trailing and the head too high and off the bit (Nos. 3 and 4).   The same thing can happen if the rider's reins are too long.

3   4
not use his legs and back.   *Incorrect halt.*

The sequence of steps at the canter.

1   *1st Beat*   2

5   *3rd Beat*   6

THE CANTER

The canter is a pace of 3 time. In the canter with the near-fore leading the sequence of legs is as follows : (1) off-hind ; (2) right diagonal; (3) near-fore.

It will be seen in these illustrations that the horse has commenced propelling himself forward with the off-hind which in No. 1 is taking all the weight (first beat). The other three legs are in the air and about to come forward. The right diagonal (off-fore and near-hind) will come to the ground next as in No. 3 (second beat). In No. 4, the off-hind has left the ground whilst the entire weight is now on the right diagonal, and the near-fore, which is the leading leg,

The sequence of steps at the canter.

is stretched forward ready to make the third beat in No. 5 and to take all the weight in No. 6. It can be seen leaving the ground in No. 7. The period of suspension, when all four feet are in the air, is shown in No. 8.

The rider must sit upright, still and down in the saddle with the body swaying as little as possible with the rhythm of the beat. Actually the rider's shoulders should be still so that it looks to the outsider as if he were sitting still and erect and swinging along as one with his horse. He must not look down to see which leg is leading neither should he round his back with his shoulders forward, nor must he allow his elbows and toes to be turned outwards.

Teaching a horse to canter.

1   2   3   4

The Aids to Canter

If the horse does not understand the canter aids he should be trotted slowly in a large circle. For a left canter, take the horse on a left circle when he would be slightly bent in that direction. The rider brings his right leg, which acts as a passive leg only to prevent the hindquarters from going to the right, back behind the girth, the left leg to the girth, and, together with a strong back and seat aid, the rider asks the horse to strike off into a left canter. As the horse progresses in his training the aids can be lighter with the inside leg taking over control. (see p. 113.)

In Nos. 1 and 2 above, the horse is trotting and the rider is drawing back his right leg preparatory to asking the horse to canter with the near-fore leading. In No. 3 he has turned the

1   2

Bracing the back to reduce pace.

Teaching a horse to canter.

5   6   7   8

horse's head slightly to the left and in No. 4 the horse is seen bringing his off-hind forward which, instead of coming forward (as in the trot) together with the near-fore, breaks that diagonal. Immediately after the period of suspension (No. 5), he drops it to the ground to become the first beat of the canter which is well demonstrated in Nos. 6, 7 and 8.

To reduce from a canter to a trot. Whilst the rider braces his back and seat muscles in a downward movement, as if all his power were being thrust out through his knees, he resists slightly with his hands whilst asking with the hand on the resisting side and the horse comes quietly back into a trot.

Illustrations Nos. 1 and 2 below show the horse cantering with the near-fore leading. In No. 1 he is on the first beat and in No. 2 his right diagonal has come to the ground. Now,

3   4

Bracing the back to reduce pace.

as the rider braces his back and seat muscles whilst resisting slightly with the hands, the horse lifts his off-hind up bringing it forward with the near-fore (No. 3) thus making it into a diagonal step when he is now trotting as in No. 4.

To reduce the pace from a canter to a walk. The rider uses much stronger seat and back aids in order to lower the haunches and drive the horse's hind-legs further under him when it will be found that he will come back easily straight into a walk pace. He must on no account be pulled back with the reins, but the hands, ever sensitive, should resist slightly as before.

Reins too long

If the rider's reins are too long he is inclined to pull his hands back into his tummy and lean forward in order to get his body out of the way. But this he cannot do, so the horse either takes no notice of these aids or falls back into a trot on

1   2   3

Disunited canter.

his forehand with his head in the air, having lost his rhythm and being off the bit.

Disunited Canter

This means a horse is cantering incorrectly, *i.e.* in a true canter one pair of laterals (*i.e.* both legs on one side) should be in advance of the other pair. In a disunited canter the horse is leading with the off-fore and near-hind or vice versa. When he does this he must be brought back into a trot at once and the correct canter recommenced. This can be seen by studying the illustrations below. In No. 1 the off-hind is on the ground; the next beat should be the right diagonal but, instead, the left laterals (near-fore and near-hind) are on the ground, followed by the off-fore and period of suspension. The student can see how awkward this horse is and how it is impossible for his rider to keep his seat in the saddle. These illustrations should be studied with those for the true canter.

It can now be understood how important it is for the rider to know the sequence of steps a horse makes in his different paces. Otherwise he cannot correct immediately any faults or evasions the horse produces.

Counter Canter

This is purely a suppling exercise for the horse. It is when the horse is cantering to the right with the left leg leading, or cantering to the left with the right leg leading. This is an excellent exercise for making the horse use his shoulders. It must not be confused with the disunited canter.

4   5   6
Disunited canter.

The sequence of steps at the gallop.

1   1st Beat   2

5   6   4th Beat

THE GALLOP

The gallop is an increased canter, therefore, as the horse lengthens his stride and stretches himself forward into a gallop the pace becomes 4 time because he cannot now put the diagonals down together, so, being broken, the sequence of legs becomes: (1) near-hind; (2) off-hind; (3) near-fore; (4) off-fore. This can be easily seen by tying handkerchiefs round one pair of diagonals.

These illustrations should be compared with those of the canter. It will be seen here that the horse has stretched himself so far forward that in the second beat (No. 3) he cannot bring the near-fore down at the same time as the off-hind, so this diagonal is broken and the near-fore makes

The sequence of steps at the gallop.

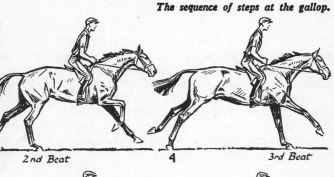

3   2nd Beat   4   3rd Beat

7   8

the third beat (No. 4) followed by the off-fore making the
fourth beat (No. 6) this leg is about to leave the ground in
No. 7, and the period of suspension (No. 8) completes the
cycle.   This horse is leading with the off-fore.

At this pace the rider should stand in his stirrups with his
seat just off the saddle and his body leaning forward.   He
must now pay great attention to his legs.   On no account
must he allow his knees and ankles to be stiff.   They should
be as if on springs and act as shock absorbers.   In this
way the rider will find he goes with his horse in great
comfort to them both and he is ready to take on any obstacle
which he may find in front of him.

The Aids.   The horse is put into a canter and then urged
forward with both legs.

JUMPING

As the rider must learn how to sit on over a jump, it is good for him to practise sitting in the jumping position whilst going round the school. He is now well versed in the correct seat for riding, so he must try standing in his stirrups for several strides at the trot with his seat just off the saddle, then coming down into the saddle again. He must keep repeating this exercise until he can stand, with bent knees—they must on no account be stiff—for several times round the school without losing his balance or hanging on by the reins. In order to accomplish this, the rider must shorten his stirrups, thus closing the hip, knee and ankle angles, otherwise he cannot keep his balance. This should be repeated at the canter. If this exercise is continually practised, the rider will find it much easier when he comes to the actual jump.

First use a pole on the ground. The rider in the jumping position goes round the school at the trot and over the pole. This can be performed several times both ways. Then a cavaletti can be used. This is a pole 9 ft. in length by 3 ins. diameter. It is bolted on to a cross-piece at either end so that it can be made three heights (10, 15 and 19 ins.) by just being rolled over.

The lowest height is used first and the pupil goes forwards and backwards over this first at the trot and then at the canter.

|← ——————— 10' ——————— →|
Jumping cavaletti.

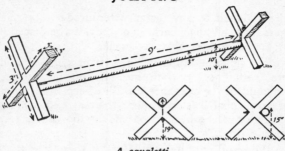

A cavaletti.

A neck strap is of great value because, if the rider gets left behind, by holding on to this he cannot jab his horse in the mouth. A free jumping horse with good manners is most essential for the beginner. The rider should remain with his seat just off the saddle, with his shoulders forward and his back straight but supple. The ankles and knees must be as if on springs with the heels well sunk, gripping with the inside of the knees and the inside of the legs, the hands and forearms forward so that an imaginary straight line can be drawn from the horse's mouth through the hands to the rider's elbows. The rider should be looking straight between the horse's ears.

After the second and third heights of the cavaletti have been negotiated with the rider still maintaining the correct position, another one can be placed 10 to 12 ft. away and the performance repeated, but this time at the canter only.

Any number of cavaletti can be used and six, 10 to 12 ft. apart, have been found to be an excellent exercise for suppling both horse and rider.

When jumping two or more cavaletti it is important for the rider to maintain the same position until he has jumped the last one and for the horse to have enough rein to allow him absolute freedom so that he can stretch and lower his head. In this way both horse and rider learn to balance themselves.

These cavaletti can be placed in all sorts of ways in order to vary the jumps : 2 close together form a spread and can be gradually widened to any distance required; one on top of two others make a "hog's back"; or they can be placed before, after, or on both sides of an obstacle.

It is of tremendous importance that the pupil should have complete confidence in both himself and his horse. The trainer should never over face him but keep him jumping all sorts of small obstacles, not more than 2 ft. 6 ins. high, in every direction at both the trot and at the canter for some considerable time.

When the pupil is quite competent at these heights, some-what larger fences can be tried, but it is best to keep them below 3 ft. 3 ins. for some time yet. A splendid gymnasium can be made with a number of fences all under this height. Spreads, small walls and gates, built-up cavaletti, etc., can be used placed at different angles. If these obstacles are continually jumped and the rider keeps them at this height, he will find his horse will jump smoothly and quietly without hotting-up, and that he himself will be sitting confidently in the saddle perfectly balanced throughout the whole exercise.

How not to jump

1. He must not thrust out his elbows with loose reins and no contact with the horse's mouth or he will lose control and the horse might run out.

The rider must not lean back allowing his legs to

How not to sit over a jump.

2. He must not "call a cab" with his right hand flung up, toes down, sitting in the saddle and looking back, as he would most likely fall off if the horse made a mistake.

3. He must not allow the horse to throw him out of the saddle so that he has only the reins with which to hold

go forward and hold on by the reins.

The position of the rider over a jump.

on by, as, again he might find himself in trouble if the horse were to swerve or to run out.

4. He must not let his legs go back with the toes pointing downwards and the knees off the saddle. Nor must the reins be held too high so that the rider's only means of remaining in the saddle is through the reins.

In illustrations Nos. 1 and 2 above it will be seen that the rider is in the "jumping position" when coming in to the fence. In Nos. 3 and 4 his body is inclined further forward in order to anticipate the thrust of the jump and to ensure non-interference with the horse's mouth. In No. 7 as the horse lands, the

The position of the rider over a jump.

rider's body assumes once more the position shown in Nos. 1 and 2. Jumping larger fences before either horse or rider is ready, is to court lack of confidence on the part of the horse and the adoption of bad positions on the part of the rider.

It is helpful to place a cavaletti 18 to 20 ft. in front of the jump which will give one full canter stride after the cavaletti and so bring the horse right at the fence.

If the rider adheres implicitly to these exercises and gets efficient in one phase before going on to the next—always remembering that perfection can only be attained by constant repetition—he will soon find jumping an exhilarating and **thrilling pastime.**

EQUIPMENT

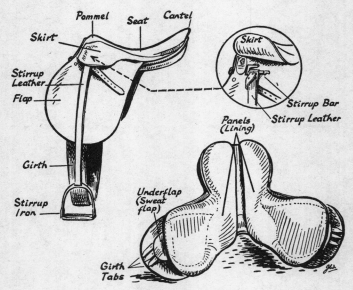

The parts of a saddle.

SADDLERY

The Saddle

The latest kind of English hunting saddle is the most comfortable as it has a central position. A central position saddle is one in which the lowest part of the seat is in the centre and usually the pommel and cantel are somewhat higher than in the old fashioned saddles. The flaps are set moderately forward with a slight roll in front of the rider's knees, which will be found to be very good for jumping as it helps to keep the leg in position.

The parts of the saddle are :—

seat	underflaps (sweat flaps)
pommel	girths
cantel	girth tabs
skirt	stirrup bars
flap	stirrup leathers and irons
panel	lining

There are three kinds of lining :—

Serge is absorbent but does not wear well and is difficult to keep clean.

Linen is easy to keep clean, dries quickly and wears much longer than serge.

Leather wears the longest and is easy to clean, but it must be kept soft especially if not in use.

There are three kinds of girths :—

Web girths do not wear very well and two should always be used as the strain on only one might cause it to break.

String girths are good as they help to prevent galling.

Leather girths are the best as they are strong and, if kept soft, are comfortable and last a long time.

The most convenient way of carrying a saddle is on the left arm with the pommel on the inside of the elbow.

To put on a saddle

The girths should be attached to the off side of the saddle and thrown over the seat with the outside of the girths on the top so when it is dirty it does not soil the saddle, and the stirrup irons run up to the top of the leathers. The saddle is now in a convenient position to be slipped quietly on to the horse's back.

Stand on the near side of the horse and place the saddle on his back well up on the withers and slide it back into its proper place. This ensures that the hair is not rubbed up the wrong way thus making it uncomfortable for the horse.

How to saddle-up a horse.

Go round to the off side, take down the girths and see that the flaps are not turned up or tucked in. If a martingale is worn, place the end of the girths through the loop of the martingale. Now return to the near side, hold the flap of the saddle up with the top of your head so that you have both hands free with which to do up the girths. These should be tightened gradually, and be sure and see that the skin is not wrinkled underneath and that the martingale, if worn, is in the centre between the horse's front legs.

It is most important to see that the pommel does not come down on the horse's withers which would happen if

Saddle too low on withers

the tree of the saddle was too wide. If it does, as shown in the illustration, it would cause him to get sore and might put him out of work for sometime.

When the tree is too wide a wither pad can be used or a folded rubber will act as a temporary measure; it must be pulled well up into the front of the saddle, not stretched flat on the horse's withers, as this, too, would cause a rub.

A wither pad is generally a piece of wool knitted into the shape of an oval bag which is stuffed with soft material. It should only be used as a temporary expediency and the saddle should be restuffed to fit as soon as possible.

Very great care must also be taken to see that the saddle in no way touches the horse's spine when the rider is mounted. Pressure here would cause considerable pain and could easily be the cause of laying the horse up for several weeks.

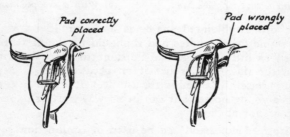

Pad correctly placed

Pad wrongly placed

A wither pad.

Bridles

There are many sorts of bridles, but only two of real value :
the snaffle and the double bridle.   The snaffle is the best
for beginners and young horses and the double bridle for
more advanced riders and for horses that have received correct
basic training.

The snaffle bridle is composed of :—

1. The head-piece and throat lash.
2. The brow-band, attached by runners to the head-piece.
3. Cheek-pieces which are stitched to the snaffle bit at one
   end and fastened to the head-piece at the other.
4. The cavesson or the dropped nose-band.
5. The reins, generally one pair, which are thick and are
   sewn on to the snaffle bit; they are sometimes fastened
   with studs or buckles.

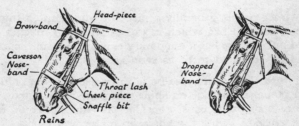

A snaffle bridle.

(a) With a cavesson nose band.   *(b) With a dropped nose band.*

The ordinary jointed snaffle is a nice mild bit which is
comfortable for the horse and it should be the first bridle to
be used as little damage can be done to the horse's mouth
should the novice rider use it on occasions as a means of
keeping himself balanced in the saddle.   It is also an excellent
bit for a young horse as it can in no way hurt or damage his
mouth if not abused.

A dropped noseband can be used in conjunction with the
snaffle and should be fitted carefully so that the front is well

above the nostrils and the back strap in the chin groove. It is passed below the bit. It is adjusted so as to prevent the horse from crossing his jaw or opening his mouth wide. This noseband prevents the horse's lips being pinched between the bit and the noseband, which is liable to occur if a cavesson noseband is used and is fitted too low and too tight. It must never be used with a double bridle.

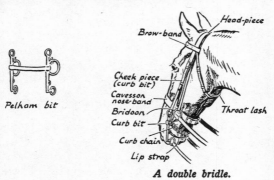

A double bridle.

The double bridle is composed of :—

1. The head-piece and throat lash.
2. The brow-band which is attached to the head-piece by runners.
3. Cheek-pieces attached at one end to the curb bit and at the other end to the head-piece.
4. Cavesson nose-band with its own head-piece.
5. Reins, the bridoon reins are usually slightly wider.
6. The bridoon with its own head-piece.
7. The curb bit with, preferably, a fixed mouth-piece.
8. The curb chain.
9. The lip strap is made in two parts, each of which is attached to the cheeks of the bit.

It is very important that this bridle should fit properly. The bridoon should lie in the horse's mouth just low enough not to cause the lips to wrinkle. The curb bit lies immediately

How to carry and put on a bridle.

below it, and the curb chain, which should be thick and flat, should lie snugly in the chin groove and be sufficiently tight to allow the cheek-pieces of the bit to be drawn back to an angle of 45 degrees with the horse's mouth. The lip strap should pass through the loose link on the curb chain and be fitted loosely.

The pelham bit is a combination of the curb and bridoon in one mouthpiece to which are attached the bridoon and curb reins thus trying to make one bit perform the duties of two. Although it appears that some horses go better in this bit, it is not one to be recommended as it is neither one thing nor the other and could never take the place of either.

A bridle can be carried by holding the buckles of the reins and the head-pieces in the right hand. If the buckles of the nose-band and throat-lash are undone, it is then ready and in position to put on the horse's head, which is done by drawing the right hand up the front of the horse's head with the left hand holding the bit after having put the reins over the horse's neck. The horse, finding a gentle pressure here, will open his mouth; then the bit can be slipped in and the head-piece quietly pushed over his ears.

PRINCIPLES OF BITTING
AND ACTION OF THE REINS

A horse will put up all sorts of evasions and act in a most outlandish manner if he is not comfortable with his bit. He will pull, get excited, throw his head about, lean on the bit or think up every sort of horror in order to try and get away from the hurt in his mouth. So the rider should ask himself the reason for all this and set about looking for it. The trouble will often be found in the mouth. He may discover a badly fitting bit that is worn and pinching the horse's lips, or he may find that the mouth is sore due to his own hands being too heavy. In either case to escape from the hurt, the horse will lean more on the bit; he will then become hard in the mouth. If he is naturally an excitable horse this will show itself in the tossing of the head and reaching at the bit.

Sometimes a horse's teeth bother him, causing him to be irritable and inattentive. The rider should have them looked at periodically and get a veterinary surgeon to file the teeth if they are too sharp. A sign of dental trouble will be seen in oats being passed undigested as the horse will be unable to use his teeth to grind them properly. It should be the object of the rider to make sure his horse is as comfortable as possible because, only in this way, will he work willingly and well. Periodic inspection of his saddle and bridle for any defects, therefore, becomes essential.

The horse must be taught to hold the bit lightly in his mouth with a relaxed jaw so that he is ready to answer the slightest aid given. This he will not do unless he has complete confidence in (a) the bit and (b) the rider's hands. His mouth is so shaped that the tongue lies in the groove made by the formation of the lower jaw, and, this being curved, it will be found that a broken bit is far more comfortable than one with a straight mouthpiece.

It is for this reason that a snaffle is used for schooling a horse. The mouthpiece is thick and broken in the middle which makes it lie nice and snug round the tongue and on the sides of the mouth and lips. It should be fitted just so high as not to wrinkle the lips. It is important for the rider to be sure that the bridle is fitted correctly. In a snaffle bridle the reins act on the sides of the mouth and the lips. As the bit folds round the tongue and is jointed in the middle, it becomes easy to ask a flexion with one rein or the other as the operating rein can act on the required side whilst, on account of the bit being broken, a steady contact can be maintained with the other rein. If a straight barred snaffle is used it becomes impossible to give a definite signal to one side or the other as the bit, being in one piece, would act as a whole.

All novice dressage competitions are ridden in snaffle bridles and it is a good bit for both hacking and jumping. It can often be seen in the hunting field, especially on young horses when it generally denotes a horse with a light mouth. By its extremely soft and accurate action it is an excellent bit to use for re-making a spoilt mouth, getting a horse to lower his head and teaching him to accept the bit.

The double bridle is not a good bit in which to school a horse but, correctly fitted and in the hands of an experienced rider it adds grace and elegance to the movements of the horse. But it should not be used until the horse has learnt to accept the bit and hold it softly in his mouth with an equal pressure on each side. It should be fitted with the bridoon as high as possible in the horse's mouth so that the lips are not wrinkled, with the bit hanging immediately below. It is good to have a fairly low port (*i.e.* arch in the centre of the bit) so that it cannot touch the roof of the horse's mouth when in action, and it should be broad so as to allow room for the tongue.

The double bridle can be severe or light according to the length of the cheek-pieces, the height of the port, the tightness of the curb-chain and the experience of the rider. The bridoon has the same action as the snaffle bridle by acting on the sides of the mouth and the lips. It controls the movements of the horse, whereas the bit acts on the tongue and bars of the mouth and resolves into a pinching action when the curb-chain comes into use. For this reason it is not a bit for the inexperienced because great damage can be done by its misuse, and it is not good for a young horse because it would restrict his action and cause him to resist if used before he understood how to accept the bit.

MARTINGALES AND HOW TO FIT THEM

Standing martingale

This is a strap attached at one end to the cavesson noseband and at the other end to the girths under the horse's belly supported by a neck-strap. The rider should learn how to get a horse's head down without resorting to a device which can only prevent him from getting his head up and never make him *keep* it down. But it is very useful on a young horse or one that has been badly trained and throws his head about and, therefore, is inclined to run away. For this reason it is of great value in the hunting field. It should be fitted at such a length as not to come into action until the horse's head becomes higher than in the correct position. This martingale should not be attached to a dropped noseband.

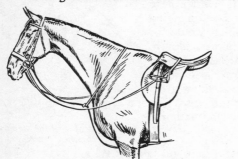

A standing martingale.   *A running martingale.*

Running martingale

One end of this is attached to the girths under the horse's belly, the other, dividing into two straps each with a ring at the end through which the reins are passed, is also supported by a neck-strap. If used on the curb-rein care must be taken to see that the rings of the martingale are not as large as those on the curb-bit, because, if they were and got over the bit rings it might cause a serious accident. It can also be used on the bridoon reins or on a snaffle bridle. It is of little use because, if fitted tight enough to come into play, it would interfere with the action of the reins and if fitted longer it would lose its value.

Irish martingale

This is two rings connected to a strap 4 to 6 inches long. The snaffle reins are passed through the rings beneath the horse's neck. Its only use is to keep the horse from throwing the reins over his head.

THE NECK-STRAP, STICKS AND WHIPS

A neck-strap could be made from a stirrup leather or any strap about that length. It is fastened round the horse's neck and is invaluable for the novice rider to hold on to, as it helps him to keep his balance instead of hanging on by the reins which would be detrimental to the horse's mouth. It is also of immense value to hold on to when learning to jump, because it gives the rider great confidence and, if he gets left behind, he does not jab the horse in the mouth.

A neck-strap for the novice to hold when jumping.

Use of Stick, Hunting Whip and Cutting Whip

An ordinary stick is usually made of cane, from 24 to 26 inches long though its thickness may vary. It should be carried below the forearm and nearly parallel to it with 4 to 6 inches protruding in front of the hand. It should be carried pointing in the direction of the horse's ear on the

A stick.   *A cutting whip.*   *A hunting whip.*

opposite side to the hand in which it is held. When it is necessary to hit a horse, it should be used behind the girths and, during its application, that hand must be taken off the rein.

The hunting whip, which is often called a crop, should never be carried without a thong and lash. The lash is the short piece of silk whipcord at the end of the thong. The hunting whip should be held at the point of balance as shown and carried in the same way as the stick with the hook to the rear pointing downwards. It can be used to prevent hounds from getting under the horse's feet, or to turn cattle and sheep thus preventing them from getting out of the field. The hook is most useful for opening and shutting gates.

The cutting whip can be of various lengths. The long ones are good for schooling and for polo, whereas the shorter variety is used for racing, and a broad piece of leather is often bound to the end as it makes a considerable noise when it comes in contact with the horse and prevents cutting or marking him.

CARE OF THE HORSE

GROOMING

Grooming is the daily attention a stable horse needs in order to keep him fit. It promotes health, keeps him in good condition, keeps him clean and improves his appearance.

Grooming kit:—

1. Hoof pick. A most important implement. It cleans out the feet and removes stones, foreign bodies, etc.
2. Dandy brush for removing heavy dirt, caked mud and dust especially on the unclipped legs of a hunter. It is particularly good for use on a horse or pony which is kept out at grass.
3. Body brush for removing scurf and dirt from the body. If used in a rotary movement it acts as a massage.
4. Curry comb for cleaning the body brush.
5. Water brush for use (damp) on the mane, tail and feet.
6. Sponge for cleaning the eyes, muzzle and dock.
7. Whisp. A twisted-up tightly woven rope of hay. For promoting circulation and massage.
8. Mane and tail comb should be used with great care as it is apt to tear out the hair and so spoil a tail. It is more often used as an implement for "pulling" the mane or tail.
9. Sweat scraper used to scrape a sweating horse and also after washing for scraping off the water.
10. Rubber is used for a final polish after grooming.

Grooming Kit.

1

The illustrations show :—

1. **The way to use a body brush.** Standing on the near-side with the owner using his left hand in a rotary movement and holding the curry comb in the right hand. (For doing the other side of the horse the reverse hands are used.) Inset is the body brush being cleaned by the use of the curry comb.

2. **Using a dandy brush on the off-hind leg.**

   Note the brush is in the right hand whilst the left hand is holding the hock; this generally prevents a horse from kicking. Sometimes the tail is held instead.

2

4

3

3. Note the position of the left hand which helps to keep the horse's leg still and the way the man is standing, which allows him freedom of movement.

4. A comb should not be used on the tail as it is inclined to pull out the hairs. It is better to brush it with a body or water brush.

5. To pick up the near-fore in order to pick out the foot, the left hand is run down from the horse's withers to his fetlock so that he is not frightened by a sudden movement. The leg is then picked up and held with the left hand whilst the foot is picked out with the pick held in the right hand.

5

A horse should be quartered (lightly groomed) before going to exercise, but should be strapped (thoroughly groomed) on return from work. As a practice it is best to pick out and inspect the feet as soon as the horse comes in from work in case he has picked up a stone or nail, as, if left, it would cause him great pain and he may then be lame and off work for some considerable time.

Though the feet should be washed, the legs must not be wetted during the operation. Mud should be allowed to dry on and then be brushed off. Washing the legs on return from work in order to get rid of the mud is frequently followed by stiffness and cracked heels and sometimes even mud fever which could incapacitate a horse for quite a while.

CLIPPING AND TRIMMING

Under natural conditions a horse will grow a thick winter coat when the weather gets cold. But, if he is required to do hard work, the coat becomes a burden and the constant sweating would result in a loss of condition. Therefore, the horse is clipped and there are several ways of doing this :—

1. *Clipped right out.* When the horse is clipped all over.

2. *Hunter clipped.* When a saddle mark and the legs are left while the rest of the horse's body is clipped. Leaving the saddle mark often prevents a horse from getting a sore back when he is not in hard condition. Leaving the legs gives the horse more protection from thorns, knocks, etc., but, if a thorn should penetrate it is much more difficult to find it in the long hair, and it makes the legs harder to dry and to keep clean.

3. *Trace clipped* is when the belly (trace high), the under side of the neck and a line up the quarters only are clipped. This is generally for a horse who is kept out at grass when he will wear a New Zealand rug ; or for a stabled horse doing light work when possibly only one blanket would be necessary to keep him warm.

Hunter clipped　　　　　　*Trace clipped*

A horse will need to be clipped 3 or 4 times during the winter. Generally the first clip would be in October followed by another one before Christmas with a third one in January. A 4th clip in February would only remove the long "cat" hairs which make a horse look so rough. These could be "singed" off, but this would not make quite such a neat job as clipping.

Trimming

The mane is trimmed by "pulling" out the hairs and thinning it to the required length. The mane can also

be "hogged" which means it is completely removed by the clippers.

A "banged" tail is one that is pulled at the top of the dock and thinned out gradually for a short way allowing the rest to flow naturally and cutting it off square about 6 inches below the hock.

A "swish" tail is also pulled at the top, but is not cut off at the bottom but ends in a long thin point.

A "banged"　　*A "swish"*
tail.　　　　*tail.*

CLOTHING

Rugs. A horse that is kept in the stables will need a rug during the summer months. It is generally made of a woollen material bound with braid of another colour. Such rugs often bear the owner's initials in the corners. There can be a roller to match, or, better still is one made of leather which is well padded where it rests each side of the spine. It is good to have a fairly high arch of metal covered with leather between these pads, which helps to prevent a horse from getting cast when rolling. The rug should fit like a loose collar round the horse's neck. If the opening is too large it will be inclined to work back over the shoulders till the top is drawn tightly across the withers and may cause a sore from pressure. Summer rugs are made of cotton and are used when it is too hot for a woollen rug in order to keep the flies away and to keep the horse clean.

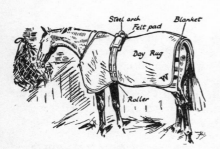

A correctly rugged-up horse.

A New Zealand rug.

Night rugs are made of hemp or jute lined with a woollen material. These rugs are used to keep day rugs clean as at night they are subject to considerable soiling when the horse lies down. If no night rugs are available, the day rug should be put on inside out.

In the winter when the horse is clipped he will need more warmth, so a blanket of pure wool is placed underneath the rug and both fastened in place with the roller. When a horse is clipped and turned out during the winter a New Zealand rug can be worn. It is made of waterproof canvas lined with wool. There are leg straps to keep the rug in place.

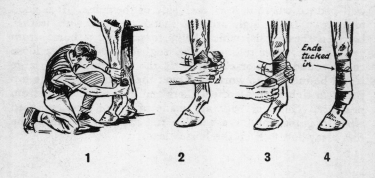

1   **2**   **3**   **4**

Stable bandages are made of wool in sets of four. They are comforting to put on after hunting, or when travelling by horse-box. They should be put on to cover as much leg as possible from the knees and hocks downwards. They should be put on loosely so as not to stop the circulation should the horse's legs swell. The illustrations show the correct way to put on these bandages :—

No. 1. The rolled-up bandage is held in the right hand with the rolled part on top and one turn is taken round the horse's leg and is held in place, under the knee, by the left hand. Nos. 2 and 3 show turns being taken round the leg clockwise. No. 4 shows the bandage, which after being taken round the fetlock, is now wound up again to the top, the flap turned in and the end fastened with a knotted bow on the outside of the leg. The ends should then be tucked in.

Knee-caps.   *Hock-boots.*

Knee-caps are worn as a protection whilst travelling.

Hock-boots are used to prevent a horse from injuring his hocks when he lies down at night, which may occur when there is insufficient bedding. This may cause a swelling which is called a capped hock.

Boots are a good thing to wear on the front legs when schooling or jumping as they prevent a horse from knocking himself. They are not good to wear out hunting or during anytime when the horse has to go through mud, as it gets inside the boots and will most likely cause a rub.

Boots.   *Working bandages.*

If a horse needs support when out hunting, racing, etc., a bandage can be used with cotton wool underneath to allow for shrinkage when the bandages get wet. Note in this case the bandages do *not* cover the fetlock joints.

A Yorkshire boot.

A Yorkshire boot is used if a horse goes too close behind and so knocks his fetlock. It is made of felt with a tape sewn across the middle, is tied round just above the fetlock joint and folded over.

A tail guard.

A tail guard is put on a tail over the top of a bandage also whilst travelling to prevent the tail from being rubbed. It is made of wool or leather with a strap at one end which is fastened to the roller to keep it in place.

How to put on a tail bandage.

To put on a tail bandage the hair must first be damped with a water brush and the hairs lying quite flat. The illustrations show how the bandage should be put on. It is important to take the bandage lower than the end of the dock so that the knot is tied below the dock. If knotted tightly on the dock it will cause the circulation to stop and white hairs would appear in the tail.

STABLING

A loose-box.

If a horse is being kept up, it is best that he should be put in a loose-box where he would get a greater measure of freedom and comfort. The box needs to be about 14 ft. by 12 ft. The door should be in two parts so that the upper portion could be hooked back and left open permitting the horse to look over the lower portion and so get plenty of fresh air. In fact the top part of the door could be taken off as it should rarely be shut. A bar is often fastened across the upper part which would prevent him from attempting to jump out.

Galvanised iron mangers are good as they are so easy to clean. The corner mangers are recommended as there are no sharp corners on which the horse can hurt himself. These mangers should be fixed into the wall breast high. Horses may also be fed from the ground in round tins or buckets attached to the wall. Hay racks are often found fitted above head level, but this is not good as, in getting the hay out, the seeds are often shaken out and get lost on the ground or get into the horse's eyes. Hay is best fed from the ground or from a hay net.

If a loose box is not available, a horse can be quite comfortable in a stall when he has once got used to being tied up. In this case the manger generally runs the breadth of the stall to which he must be tied and there is, as a rule, a place for water. Sometimes a hay rack at breast level is incorporated as well. A horse in a stall must wear a headcollar to which is attached a head-rope fastened to the back "D" of the nose-band. This head-rope is passed through the ring on the manger and secured to a log which is placed at the end of the rope so that it just touches the ground when the horse stands up to the manger. This prevents him from getting his leg over the rope and becoming cast; it is made long enough to allow him to lie down.

A ring at breast level for tying the horse up to the manger and another at eye level for short racking him is very essential.

A stall.

To short-rack a horse means to tie him up to a ring on the wall, at eye level. This is to restrict his movement so that he cannot turn round and bite when being groomed. It also prevents him from lying down after being groomed.

It is most important that a horse should be tied up with a quick-release knot so that, in case of an emergency, he can be released immediately.

A horse should have as much air as possible; therefore, the top half of all loose-box and stable doors must be kept open, also all windows except where they might cause a draught. In cold weather it is better to add an extra rug or place a sack over the loins under the top rug, rather than to close the windows.

Bedding

Wheat straw is the best bedding for a horse; it makes a warm comfortable bed, is easily handled and permits free drainage. Also this kind of bedding is valuable manure, and could, therefore, be a source of income.

Oat straw can also be used, but, being more palatable, horses are inclined to eat it. Barley straw should not be used as the awns on the ears are prickly and irritate the skin, also, if eaten, they might cause colic.

Peat moss is popular with some and makes a good bed, but care must be taken to see that the droppings are picked up and all damp parts dug out or else the owner may get trouble with the horse's feet. With this kind of bedding there is no sale as manure and it is important to block up all drains before putting down the peat or else the pipes will get filled in.

Shavings make quite a good bed but it is bad manure and it must constantly be kept clean. Sawdust is not good as it is inclined to clog and overheat which is bad for the horse's feet.

FEEDING AND WATERING

Feeding horses is an art which some people seem to have and others have not. A horse's natural food is grass which he grazes off and on throughout most of the day and night. Having a very small stomach it should not be over-loaded and those who look after him should study his appetite and feed him accordingly. All the same there are a few rules which should be more or less adhered to :—

1. Feed little and often in imitation, as far as possible, of the natural method.

2. Feed plenty of bulk food (hay) so that the digestive organs are kept occupied.

3. Feed according to the work done. Increase the corn if the demands of work are heavy, reduce it if they become light and knock it off if the horse has to be laid up.

4. Water before feeding so that undigested food is not washed out of the stomach. When water is kept continuously in the box a horse will frequently take a short drink during or after a feed, but, as this does not amount to a long draught, it will not hurt him.

5. Change the diet occasionally. A horse gets tired of eating the same thing day-in and day-out unless it is grass.

6. Do not work him hard immediately after a full meal. The stomach lies next to the chest so it will press on the lungs when full and prevent the lungs from expanding freely.

7. Feed clean and good quality food only. Musty fodder will not only affect the horse's condition, but may well prove harmful to his wind.

Oats are the best feed for a horse and the quantity he consumes must depend upon the amount of work he is doing. A hunter could have 15 to 16 lb. of oats a day in four different

**feeds. A hack possibly 5 to 8 lb. according to his excitability.
Oats may be fed whole, bruised or boiled. Bruised (or
crushed) oats are mostly used as this aids the digestion, but
whole oats may be better for horses that are doing fast work.**

Barley should be used with discretion. Boiled barley is
sometimes added to the diet of a delicate feeder with good
results. Barley must always be steamed or boiled as given
in its natural state it is very heating and indigestible.

Beans are very nutritious but are very heating and should
be fed only in small quantities.

Chaff is chopped hay and should be mixed with all feeds as
it provides bulk and prevents the horse from bolting his food.

Wheat if uncooked is bad food and should be avoided as it
is indigestible.

Bran is a very valuable article of forage for horses. Fed
dry it is added to and mixed with the oats and chaff which form
bulk. Fed wet as a bran mash it has laxative properties and
is thus of special value to a sick horse or to one who is tempor-
arily thrown out of work. It is good to feed a bran mash on
Saturday night when the horse has a rest on the Sunday.
To make a bran mash, fill a stable bucket about two-thirds
full of bran, pour boiling water over it and stir well. Then
cover with a sack and feed when cool enough to eat. The
mash can be made more appetising if a little salt, some boiled
linseed or a handful of oats is added.

Linseed is fed to horses to improve condition and to give
gloss to the coat. In its natural form it is very indigestible
so it must be prepared with care. Place about $\frac{1}{2}$ pint of linseed
in a saucepan in the evening, cover with water and allow to
soak all night with the lid on, add a little more water, bring
it to the boil and allow to simmer for 2 or 3 hours. Set it
aside and allow to cool, when it will become jelly. It can
then be added to the evening meal, especially to a mash.

Gruel is good for horses after hunting or a very hard day's
work. It acts as a pick-me-up. To prepare gruel place a
double handful of oatmeal in a bucket, pour on boiling water

and stir well. It should be given cool and should be thin enough for the horse to drink.

Carrots are a nice change. They are best left unwashed and sliced lengthways.

Swedes and mangels are most appetising after Christmas and can be fed in the same way as carrots.

Salt in small quantities is a necessary addition to a horse's feed. A teaspoonful can be put into each feed or a lump of rock salt kept in the manger.

Hay is the bulk food and is the substitute for grass. There are many kinds, the chief being :—sainfoin, clover, mixture and meadow. Of these probably sainfoin is the most nutritious, clover hay is rich and for a hunter is better mixed with meadow hay. Mixture is seed hay obtained from a ley and meadow hay is from a field of permanent grass. Hay less than 6 months old should be avoided. Feed from 10 to 15 lb. of hay a day.

A horse needs from 23 to 25 lb. of bulk per day, therefore, the more hay he gets the less corn he needs and vice versa.

Watering

The importance of clean and adequate water cannot be overstressed. Nothing affects the condition of a horse so quickly as faulty water conditions. It is, therefore, most essential that the horse has a constant supply of fresh water.

In a loose-box it is best to keep in one of the corners a bucket full of water which must be kept constantly replenished. If the horse is kept in a stall and there is no place for a bucket water must be given to him frequently and always before each meal. If a horse is turned out to grass it is most important that he should have a stream or running water in a trough to drink from. During frosty weather the ice must be kept broken.

Buckets made of oak are the best for water as they are heavy and the horse is unlikely to knock them over or damage himself with them. They must be kept clean.

SHOEING

The usual type of shoe for hunters and hacks is a concave fullered pattern shoe with small calkins and wedge heels on the hind shoes. There are usually 7 nails, 4 on the outside and 3 inside.

A concave shoe has the inside of the ground surface hollowed out so that it is narrower than the foot surface, the advantage being that it is lighter and creates less suction and is, therefore, less likely to be lost in deep going. When the shoe is fullered it has a groove on the ground surface in which the nail holes are placed. This gives a better foothold and prevents slipping.

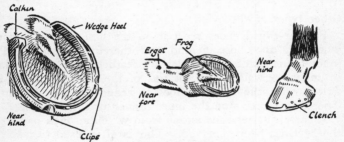

A concave fullered shoe.

Calkins are formed by turning down the end of the heel on the hind feet at right angles, thus, the projection, being forced into the ground, gives a good grip. When calkins are fitted to the outer heel of the shoe, the inner heel is narrowed and thickened (wedge heel) so that it brings them level. The object of using a wedge heel on the inside is to lessen the chance of brushing.

Clips are used to keep the shoe in place and to prevent it from being forced backwards. One clip is placed on the toe of the front shoes and two (one on each side of the toe) on the hind shoes. This latter is to avoid over-reaching.

After the nails have been driven home, the ends that project are called clenches. These are pinched off and the parts that remain are hammered firmly into the wall of the hoof.

A horse should be shod about once a month on account of the growth of the hoof, but if the old shoes are still good enough they should be taken off and replaced. This is called remove.

Points to look for to see if a shoe requires attention :—

1. See that the clenches are not up.

2. See that the shoe has not slipped, *i.e.*, that it is not projecting anywhere beyond the walls of the foot, or spread.

3. See that the shoe is not loose.

4. See that the toe is not nearly worn through.

Other types of shoe

Feather-edged shoes are put on the hind feet of a horse who goes too close behind and therefore brushes. The inner branches of such shoes are feathered and fitted close in under the wall so that the risk of the horse knocking his fetlock with the opposite foot is reduced to a minimum. There are no nails on the inner branch of these shoes.

A three-quarter shoe is one from which an inch or two of the heel has been removed. This is often used to take the pressure off the seat of corn.

A tip is one that is not more than half the length of the full shoe. This is used when a horse is turned out to prevent his hoofs from breaking. It is sometimes used to increase frog pressure by bringing the frog (see illustration, page 81) on to the ground.

Feather-edged Shoe   *Three-quarter Shoe*   *Grass Tip*

CARE OF SADDLERY

A saddle horse.

Good saddlery is very expensive. It is, therefore, essential that it should be well looked after. Everything should be carefully inspected periodically and any loose stitches or defects attended to. Stirrup leathers should occasionally be shortened from the buckle end so as to bring wear into fresh holes.

Leather gets dry and cracks unless kept pliable with oil or fat. Linseed or mineral oil should not be used as it becomes hard. Castor oil, dubbin, olive oil, neatsfoot oil and glycerine are good for leather, particularly when it is not being used. The ordinary glycerine saddle soap is the best for regular use.

Cleaning

Place the saddle on a saddle horse and strip it, *i.e.*, remove girths, stirrup leathers and irons, then clean the lining which may be of leather, linen or serge. Remove all dirt and dried sweat from the inside of the saddle and hold it, pommel down, over a bucket and wash with cold or luke-warm water. Dry leather lining with a chamois leather after which apply the saddle soap. Two sponges must be used, one for cleaning off the dirt and the other, which should not get wet, for the soaping when it is better to wet the soap and rub it on the sponge rather than vice versa. If the lining is of linen, sponge off the dirt and stand the saddle up to dry. It must not be placed near a hot fire or a hot radiator. If it is a serge lining it must be scrubbed, dried and then well brushed with a dandy brush.

The saddle is now replaced on the saddle horse, the seat, flaps and underneath all thoroughly washed with cold water and then dried with a leather. Be sure that all the black greasy marks called jockeys are removed, then with the soap sponge as dry as possible liberally soap the seat, flaps and all underneath. Finally clean all metal work with metal polish and cover the saddle with a rubber and put away in a dry place.

The simplest way of putting up a saddle is to have a bracket made about 18 inches long and attach it to the wall of the saddle room at a convenient height.

Stirrup leathers and leather girths should be treated in the same way. If the soap sponge is too wet lather will appear in the holes of the leathers and, unless cleaned out with a match, will accumulate dirt. With folded leather girths a strip of flannel soaked in neatsfoot oil placed inside the folds keeps it soft and in good condition.

String and web girths should be brushed daily and washed occasionally with soap and water.

Irons should be of the best quality metal, steel or stainless steel being the best. To clean they should be washed and dried thoroughly. Clean all steel with metal polish and silver sand and shine with a dry rubber. Clean other metal with metal polish.

A saddle, stirrups, girths and leathers "put up."

Bridles

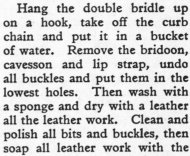

Hang the double bridle up on a hook, take off the curb chain and put it in a bucket of water. Remove the bridoon, cavesson and lip strap, undo all buckles and put them in the lowest holes. Then wash with a sponge and dry with a leather all the leather work. Clean and polish all bits and buckles, then soap all leather work with the soap sponge paying particular care to the underside of the leather. Put the bridle together, having thoroughly dried and polished the curb-chain, with all buckles back in their correct holes with their strap ends run into their keepers and runners.

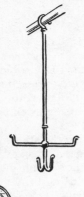

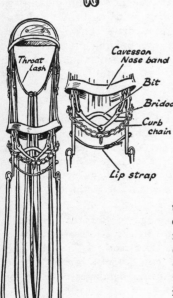

Throat lash

Cavesson Nose band

Bit

Bridoon

Curb chain

Lip strap

To put up the bridle run the throat lash through the ends of the reins, put the nose-band right round the outside of the cheek pieces and hook the curb-chain in front of the bit. Hang up on a half-moon shaped fixture in the saddle room.

A double bridle "put-up" and (above) hook for use when cleaning.

COMMON AILMENTS

Wounds

Clean the wound as soon as possible by clipping the hair in the vicinity and then wash with water and a mild solution of antiseptic. Soap and water is excellent or it can be sprayed with a hose-pipe. Then apply penicillin. Dry boric powder is also good. If it is possible to bandage, cover the wound with a piece of lint and gauze-covered cotton wool and bandage lightly so as to allow room for subsequent swelling which may take place.

If the wound is deep, after having given the above first-aid, it is as well to get the veterinary surgeon in case it needs stitching and possibly to give an injection against lock-jaw.

If the bleeding is excessive and is spurting bright red it is from an artery which calls for immediate control either by tight bandaging of the wound or by applying pressure above the wound. A pebble so placed inside a handkerchief as to bring pressure on the artery above the wound is an emergency method.

Girth Galls and Sore Backs

These are caused by the horse being in soft condition and appear as a rub on the soft skin behind the elbow or other places where there is friction or undue pressure. Work must stop, but the horse can be exercised in-hand. Dress by fomentation or apply kaolin paste for a few days and harden off with salt and water or methylated spirit.

Brushing

This is caused by hitting one leg against the other, generally the fetlock. It may be due to bad conformation, faulty action, badly fitting shoes or to over-work. Fit a feather-edged shoe and, if the horse still knocks himself, boots may have to be worn, or, if hunting, bandages with cotton wool underneath.

Stone or nail in foot

This must be picked out with a hoof-pick, but if one is not available, the butt end of a knife or any kind of blunt instrument can be used. If it has penetrated the sole, send for a veterinary surgeon as the damage done may be considerable.

Cracked heels

This is a chapping of the skin behind the pasterns due generally to neglect after washing the legs. It may produce severe lameness. Treat with pads of cotton wool soaked in lead lotion and bandage. Afterwards dry off with boracic powder.

Corns

These are bruises of the sole in the heel region, just beneath the heel of the shoe. If a corn is suspected, consult the farrier who will remove the shoe and decide on what action to take.

Colic

This is a pain in the stomach indicated by general uneasiness, off feed, looking round at the flanks, kicking at the stomach and getting up and down. Give the horse a colic drink, which should be from the veterinary surgeon, keep him walking about and do not let him get down, keep him warm with an extra rug. If he does not get better within a couple of hours, expert assistance must be sent for.

Colds

This shows as a yellow or white discharge from both nostrils. It can be caused by bad ventilation, lack of fresh air or long confinement in a stuffy horse-box, etc. It is contagious and the horse should, if possible, be isolated. Stop work, give him plenty of fresh air, but do not let him be in a draught, rug him up and put on bandages for warmth. Feed off the ground with bran mashes. Steam the head and clear the nostrils with cotton wool which must be burnt.

For other complaints such as splints, spavins, curb and thoroughpin get expert advice.

The Medicine Cupboard should contain :—

A clinical thermometer.	A bottle of disinfectant.
A pair of blunt ended surgical scissors.	A bottle of tincture of iodine.
Calico bandages 3″ and 4″.	A pint bottle of lead lotion.
Small packets of lint.	A jar of cough electuary.
A 1 lb. roll of cotton wool.	A tin of boracic powder.
A colic drink	A tin of kaolin paste.

Always keep your horse's head towards hounds.

RECREATION AND SPORT

HUNTING

Every horse capable of being ridden is suitable for some rider to hunt in some country. It depends upon the country the rider wishes to hunt in, his capabilities as a horseman and his age and weight, as to what sort of horse he would require for hunting. In grass country such as Leicestershire, a well bred galloping horse is required, whereas, in a hilly country such as one finds in the North or in Devonshire a stocky horse would be found more useful. But in any case, the better the horse is trained, the more the rider will enjoy his sport.

The horse must be groomed and fed at least one hour before starting to the meet and the time of departure should be decided by allowing for travelling at about 5 miles an hour. Leave a quarter of an hour extra so that, after having arrived, there is time to loosen the girths after dismounting and give the horse a chance to stale. Before leaving home it is as well to prepare the evening hay net and bran mash and, if possible, a drink of gruel.

When the time for moving-off at the hunt has arrived, check your saddlery, tighten the girths and mount. Be careful always to turn your horse's head towards hounds so that he cannot kick them if he happens to be fresh and always leave plenty of room for them to pass. A careless rider may do a lot of damage by allowing his horse to kick hounds.

Remember that you are now under orders from the Field Master and his directions must be obeyed without question. Do not stand gossiping at the covert side, but stand still, listen and watch what the hounds are doing. In this way you can be one of the first to get away when hounds break covert and the fox has been hollared away.

A careless rider can do a lot of damage.

Finally, thank the Master for an enjoyable day when you wish him goodnight. Now your object is to get your tired horse home as soon as possible so loosen the girths and jog off on a loose rein. If you pass a stream the horse can have a short drink but he must then jog on and not be allowed to get cold. Try and get home at about the same pace as you went to the meet, but walk the last mile so that he comes in cool. On arrival home, first wash out the horse's feet to make sure there is no stone or nail in them, then remove the bridle and lift the saddle up(replacing it in the same place) and throw a rug over him. Now shut the door and encourage the horse to stale by whistling or shaking some straw underneath him.

Fetch the gruel, add some lukewarm water to it and give it to him to drink, then hang up the hay net. The horse must now be dried off and made as comfortable as possible. Be sure and look for thorns in his legs and it is comforting for a tired horse to have all his legs done up in stable bandages.

Now give him his bran mash and leave him to eat it. He must be looked at again later on to be sure that he has not broken-out and, if he is dry and contented, he may be left for the night after a dry feed and filling up his hay net.

Correct clothes for Hunting

1. Scarlet or black hunting coat, white breeches and top boots with mahogany or scoured tops, white stock, hunting waistcoat and top hat.

2. Black or dark grey hunting coat with drab or yellow breeches, black butcher boots (without tops), white stock, hunting waistcoat and top hat.

3. Ratcatcher hacking coat, drab breeches, butcher or brown boots, stock or tie and bowler hat.

4. Ladies Side Saddle. Black or navy blue habit, top hat, white stock, veil, black butcher boots and a spur.

Brown leather or washleather gloves should always be worn and a spare pair of string or wool gloves kept under the

saddle flap in case of rain.   A hunting whip should be carried.
Blunt spurs must be worn with Nos. 1 and 2, but are optional
with No. 3.   With some hunts ladies are allowed to wear
hunting caps instead of bowlers or top hats if riding astride;
it is also in order for ladies to wear black or dark blue hacking
coats when riding this way.

A few "do's" and "don'ts" :—

DO

1. Shut gates so that farm stock cannot get out.
2. Ride the headlands if you have jumped into a field of seeds.
3. Obey any orders given you by a member of the Hunt Staff.
4. Be polite and help catch a loose horse in the case of a fall.
5. Get off your horse at the end of a sharp run or, if there is not time, turn his head to the wind to help him breathe.

DON'T

1. Over-ride hounds.
2. Get in front of the Master or Huntsman.
3. Jump on to hounds.
4. Ride across seeds.
5. Jump fences when hounds are not running.
6. Gallop through a herd of cows or a flock of sheep.
7. Ride your horse to a standstill, you may want him again later.
8. Interfere with hounds unless asked to.

Correct clothes for hacking.

HACKING

One might define hacking as "riding for the pure pleasure of riding." In these days there are many people living in towns who like to get out into the country at week-ends when they can indulge their taste for riding at the same time as enjoying the fresh air by hacking in the nearby country.

With the fast running traffic which never seems to stop or to slow down for horses, riders wishing to go out hacking must certainly have control of their horses and a knowledge of how to act in an emergency. If a car comes along which is obviously not going to slow down, the rider must at once get a very strong hold of his horse with both legs, he must get to the right side of the road and hold the left rein with slightly more contact than the right one. So, whilst the legs keep the horse going forward, the reins guide him. The left rein slightly turns his head towards the approaching car and keeps him from swinging round to the right and turning his quarters into the car. Of course he may try to nap the other way, but it is safer to keep the horse's head turned in the direction of a moving obstacle. On the other hand, should the motorist slow down or halt, the rider should acknowledge this politeness by raising his arm in salute.

Ride with the traffic.

If a horse is frightened of a stationary object, he should be quietly urged up to look at it so that he may realise that it will not hurt him. When he has smelt it, he will probably walk past quite happily without making any more fuss. If he refuses to go near, he must then be made to pass by the use of very strong leg-aids to push him forwards and this time the horse's head should be turned away from the object of fright with an extra strong pressure of the leg on this side. This has the effect of bending the horse away from the thing he is shying at and he is so busy trying to look at it that he has passed the object of fright before he realizes it.

If hacking across country the rider must remember to get permission from the owner of the land before riding over it. He must shut all gates and take care

Turn the horse's head away from a stationary object.

not to ride amongst cattle or sheep.   He must not ride across seeds or damage growing crops.

Do not ride too near people on a road so as to frighten them or to splash them with mud.   Finally, do not do any fast work on the road as it is bad for the horse's feet; and be sure to bring your horse in cool and not excited.   Otherwise he will keep breaking-out for hours afterwards.

Clothes to wear hacking

Tweed coat.
Any shade of fawn or brown breeches.
Brown or butcher boots.
Bowler, soft or hard cap or felt hat.
Breeches and gaiters or jodhpurs.
Collar and tie or coloured stock.
Stick or cutting whip.
Spurs.
Gloves.
   (*The last three are optional*).

SHOWING

A show horse needs a lot of preparing before he is ready to enter the Ring and here the dressage student will have the advantage because the horse must be schooled to walk, trot, canter and gallop when asked.   If the horse will do all these nicely and come back in hand still maintaining a light contact with the bit, he will win more prizes than better looking horses that are not so well trained.

The horse must be schooled to perform these movements willingly and at the slightest indication of the rider; he must also be physically fit so that, however hard the ground, his legs will be strong and hard enough not to trouble him.

The rider must now study his horse, because it depends so much on his mental outlook as to when to arrive at the show. If he is of an excitable nature it is as well to get to the show ground early when the horse should be ridden about very quietly and calmly, perhaps for one, maybe for two, hours.   It

Stand your horse lengthways to the side of the Ring.

is of no use to gallop an excitable horse about as it will only hot him up more, but quietly trot, canter, trot in and out of other horses, as near to the Ring as you can get and, as soon as he starts hotting-up, come back to a walk and then start all over again. Good, long, slow work on the lunge is often a better way of getting an animal quiet as it has a very soporific effect on most horses. This is called riding-in and, if this part of the work is carried out properly and the horse enters the Ring in a good frame of mind, half the rider's worries are over and it is then up to the judges. If he is a quiet, solemn horse he may need only half an hour's riding-in. There can be no hard and fast rule but it is always better to be at the show early so that there is extra time to spare if the horse needs more work.

An ordinary hunting saddle is best with not too exaggerated knee rolls as they are inclined to make the horse look short in front. At the same time the flaps should not be straight because this sort of saddle is uncomfortable to sit on and it is most important for the judges to be comfortable. An ordinary double bridle should be used. Boots, bandages, martingales and blinkers are not allowed.

When once in the ring the rider must obey orders from the ring steward and never argue. He must always be polite but he should try and get into a good position so that, when he passes in front of the judges, there is no other horse blocking their view. The rider can be firm and keep this position but he should not push other riders out of the picture in order to gain a better place for himself.

Horses will now be called in and formed up in a line for the judges to ride those they choose. During the time of waiting it is as well to see that your horse is standing well and looking nice as one never knows when a judge will take a hasty look in his direction. After both judges have ridden him, the saddle must be taken off and now he can be smoothed down with a rubber. Take the reins over his head and lead him up in front of the judges but remember that there are a lot of spectators, so make the horse stand lengthways to the side of the Ring so that all can see him. He must now be led away at a walk for some 20 yards, turned round and trotted back. When turning round the horse should be pushed round to the right, as he will then have his hind-legs well under him and be ready for the trot back. There is a great art in doing this and it should be practised at home so that the horse knows what he has to do and does it well.

If our rider is lucky and wins, he should thank the judge or whoever presents him with the rosette. Likewise, if he is 2nd, 3rd or even lower down, he must not show annoyance but be grateful for small mercies. Luckily all judges do not think alike and it is well to lose with a good grace and congratulate the winner.

Clothes

The instructions in the show schedule should be carefully read so as to be sure of wearing the right clothes and to turn out as smart as possible. If nothing is stated in the regulations, the rider may wear ratcatcher costume (see page 91) with a stick instead of a hunting whip. It is advisable to have a pair of string gloves available in case of wet weather.

Study each jump carefully.

COMPETITIVE JUMPING

As in Showing, the riding-in for Jumping Competitions is of great importance. The horse must be got into the ring well suppled-up and in the right frame of mind. Again, the amount of work this entails depends entirely on the mentality of the horse. Some need a lot of work and some need less. A practice fence should be jumped once or twice, but not too often.

As competitors are always allowed to walk round the course before a competition, this is an opportunity which should never be missed. In show jumping each jump should be studied with care and a mental note made of the distance between obstacles so that the rider can decide whether he should go fast and take only two strides or pull back the horse to a slower pace and make him take three strides. He must also note the best angle at which to jump the fence, and, in the case of a speed test, which is the quickest way he can take it with safety. In cross-country competitions it is just as important to walk the course to note the best take-offs in front of a fence, the best angle at which to jump and the easiest way for the horse. Sometimes it is not always the shortest way that is the quickest. If the ground is heavy and badly poached it may be best to go round as it would take less out of the horse than galloping through a heavy patch. If, as in this picture, there is a drop on the landing side, the rider can decide at what point it is best to land with less likelihood of the horse pecking. It is also important to note the time allowed so as not to lose unnecessary marks by being over time.

It is not in good taste to question the judge's decisions; he has been asked for his opinion and gives it in good faith. If the rider considers that a mistake has been made he is at liberty to lodge a complaint at the secretary's office in the correct manner.

Nothing is more objectionable to the public than to see a rider knocking a horse about either in the ring or outside. It does no good to the horse and ruins the rider's reputation. The points on the rowels of the spurs should be filed down. It is detrimental to the good name of this sport to see a horse come out of the ring with his flanks bleeding.

The clothes for competitive jumping are the same as for showing.

MORE ADVANCED HORSEMANSHIP

DIFFERENT TEMPERAMENTS IN HORSES

Perhaps the most interesting part of riding is that every horse is different and the rider should remember this and be able to make a complete and absolute study of each horse he has to train. Some horses are very nervous and highly strung. With this sort of horse great patience is essential. Because his nervous system reacts so quickly, and possibly violently, not only to outside influences but to the actions of his rider, he must be handled with very great tact. The daily lessons should not be too long, and the rider would be wise to take him very quietly through his exercises. If any strong influence is forced upon him, he would be inclined to hot up immediately and produce every sort of evasion possible. For this reason it is essential for the rider to be able to feel the movements of his horse and, as he gets to know the horse better, he can often anticipate a resistance and break it down almost before it has appeared. This kind of horse will always be difficult to produce, but, having once got his confidence, he will most likely give of his best when required and produce an extra brilliance not possible with his more phlegmatic brother.

The rather lazy horse produces an altogether different problem. He is most likely a heavier sort of horse of a more common type. The rider must now entirely change his tactics. This horse must be sent on at a good strong trot, but never so fast as to make him lose his rhythm and run; he must trot with a long level stride. Directly the horse quickens his stride or takes unlevel steps, he should be brought back to a slower pace and the rider must then try again to get him to lengthen his stride. With this horse great firmness should be applied. He must never be allowed to slop along at his own pace, but be made to work and use himself properly.

Then we have horses with all sorts of mouths. The hard-mouthed horse is one that really lies on his bit and either throws up his head and runs away or lowers it charging off equally fast and out of control. To cure this is a long and tedious process. The horse must be worked in a snaffle bridle and never allowed to lie on the bit. Each time he attempts to do so the rider should bring him back with a half-halt into a slower pace, the rein on the resisting side (see p. 104) given and the horse allowed to proceed as before. But the moment he takes the bit too strongly the same process must be repeated again and again until the horse will go with a light contact on both reins and no increase of pace. This may take a long time but the rider must exercise a lot of patience and neither expect nor ask too much. While this lesson is being learnt, it is often very beneficial for an impatient horse to have a lot of very small jumps dotted about the schooling ground and suddenly ask him to pop over one or the other of these out of a trot. It is surprising how quickly he will come to jumping in a perfectly quiet and unexcited manner. He will then be well on his way to learning obedience.

Another sort of awkward horse is one who will not go up to the bit but lowers his head bringing it nearer and nearer to his chest. This is also a difficult horse to deal with and the trainer will have to be very soft with his hands whilst strong with his legs and seat so that the horse is pushed forward. In so doing the head will come up, but the rider will find that the horse will take every opportunity of evading the bit again in the same way. Here again it requires a repetition of the strong leg and back-aids. Once more tact from the rider must play a great part because he must persuade the horse that the bit is not going to hurt him and that he will be more comfortable holding it lightly in his mouth with a nice head carriage, rather than carrying his head in what must be an uncomfortable position in order to drop the bit. Often these horses become artful if not corrected in the early stages; they will toss their heads and break into a canter or make little jumps. In fact they will invent any little nonsense in order to evade doing what has been asked. It is, therefore, important to be very firm with them in the beginning of their schooling.

There are many other kinds of horses. Those who carry their heads too high or too low or to one side or the other. All these are faults which have to be corrected. But no *force* should ever be used. If a horse is forced into a certain position by a strong hand and leg-aid or by a strong bit, the result will be seen at once in a restricted action. The horse must be *shown* where to put his head and made to carry himself. He will then do it on his own with great fluency.

It will now be seen how important it is to study and understand a horse if the ultimate aim is to produce an elegant and obedient animal. Exactly how far this training goes must depend upon the sphere of life in which the rider is interested and the capabilities of his trainer Whether it is for hunting, racing, polo, show jumping, showing, cross-country competitions or dressage, the basic principles of training are the same. The race horse requires the minimum amount of schooling and the dressage horse the maximum.

It will most certainly be found that every horse will benefit by correct dressage training. His muscles will be more developed, he will be better balanced, he will have more control of his own body, he will be supple and, last but by no means least, he will be *obedient*.

The trainer will be able to assess his capabilities as the horse proceeds with his training. If the horse goes freely forward with a nice level rhythm at the trot with plenty of activity, and has a well balanced and elastic canter with the motive power driving from behind, then he can be sure that his training is on the right lines. But if the horse goes unlevel behind when asked to extend at the trot, or when changing direction or turning a corner and takes short stumpy strides at the canter, then his training has been incorrect. Success depends on this early training. If it is hurried or incorrect, bad habits will be formed which will be difficult to eradicate. But, if great care and patience is taken in the initial stages, as the work proceeds it will be found that the more advanced exercises will come without difficulty.

BASIC TRAINING

The basic training consists of making the horse supple and completely obedient to the rider's wishes. He should be on the bit with a light contact at all times at all paces. Let us consider what this means because it plays a most important part in the training of a horse. To be on the bit means the horse is holding the bit lightly in his mouth with a relaxed jaw, taking an even pressure on both sides of his mouth; and he should remain like this just so long as the rider keeps contact with the bit. It means that the horse must not resist with his mouth. If he does, it is felt throughout his body by way of his neck and spine, ending in the quarters becoming high and the hind legs thrust far out behind him. This means he is stiff; he will lose his rhythm and, when asked to turn a corner or move in another direction, he will fall in on to his shoulder and be completely unbalanced. In order to lower the quarters and get the hind legs well under the horse he must lower his head and not give any resistance anywhere and must always go forward.

It will now be seen how important the mouth is. Through it all evasions occur and all stiffness is produced.

A horse "on the bit."　　　*A horse "resisting the bit."*

A good schooling bit is shown here (p. 104). It is an ordinary jointed snaffle with side pieces which prevent the bit from

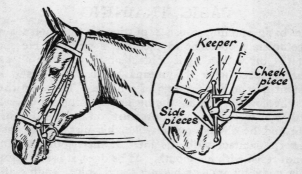

A good snaffle bridle.

No. 1. The horse answering the rein on the "soft" side.

No. 2. The horse resisting the rein on the "hard" side.

(*a*) rubbing the sides of the mouth, and (*b*) being pulled through the mouth to one side or the other. Note also the small keeper fastening the side-pieces of the bit to the cheek-pieces of the bridle. This prevents the bit from turning over in the mouth and is, therefore, always in the same position.

It will be found that all horses are stiffer on one side than on the other. Thus, the rider must discover which is the stiff side and which is the soft side. To do this when the horse is walking, he picks up the left rein only (see No. 1); if the horse answers immediately by turning his head to the left and moving off in that direction it is pretty certain that is the soft side. The rider now drops this rein and picks up the right rein and he finds that the horse will not turn his head to the right, but moves in that direction with a stiff jaw and neck, keeping his head straight or even turning it slightly to the left (see No. 2).

He has now established that the horse is stiff on the right side, which means that the muscles of the neck are longer on that side and shorter on the left (soft) side by being continually bent in that direction. The rider now sets about making the horse equally supple on both sides.

The walk is a dangerous pace at which to work as impulsion can be lost. If much work is done at this pace, except briskly walking-on with a long rein, in the early stages of training the walk is liable to become a two-time pace, impulsion is lost, the horse takes a shorter stride and the rider finds great difficulty in producing an extended walk when required. It is important to make the horse walk out on a long rein at this pace. He therefore proceeds at the sitting trot and performs a large circle to the right. He takes a light but firm contact with the left hand (soft or hollow side). And now, as the horse resists the right rein, the rider does not take a continual contact with this rein, but asks for a flexion by a slight tightening of the fingers. The motion must *not* be backward, but should be slight and quick as the squeezing of a sponge.

This aid must be supported by the legs with the right leg giving a stronger aid at the same time as the right hand is asking.   The action is repeated until the horse has answered by accepting the bit lightly on both sides of his mouth.

By repeating this aid the horse will soon give with his lower jaw and become soft when the rider must immediately sit very still and quiet with polite, soft hands until the horse resists again, when the same squeezing-water-out-of-a-sponge action should come into play once more.   When the horse is going nicely the rider can then change the rein and repeat the same aids on the other hand   In this way it will be found that the horse will resist the right rein less and less until he becomes soft on both sides taking an even pressure on both sides of his mouth.   Should he be stiff on the left, the aids are reversed.

During this time the rider should pay great attention to the level pace of his horse.   It will be found that many horses will

The horse must lengthen his stride and not quicken it.

take a shorter stride at the trot with one hind-leg thus giving the impression of not going level; this happens chiefly when changing direction or pace.   Although it is of great import-ance for the horse to go on at this stage of his training, he must not be asked more than he is capable of giving at a level pace.   Therefore, the trot must be reduced until the horse takes level strides, when once more he can be asked gradually to extend himself, but it is important that he should *lengthen* his stride and not *quicken* it.

A good exercise is to ask for a few slightly extended paces, come back to a more collected pace, extend again and so on. In this way the horse learns balance and rhythm and it is the beginning of obtaining true collection and also true extension. This exercise is best performed on a large circle to commence with as it is easier for a horse to keep his balance than on a straight line.

If the horse carries his head too high (see No. 1) it can be lowered by repeating exactly the same aids as those for getting

The horse must be "asked" to lower his head.

him to relax his jaw, *i.e.*, the squeezing-of-the-sponge action on the *stiff* side. It will soon be found that, as the horse relaxes his jaw he lowers his head at the same time (see No. 2).

In the case of too low a head-carriage, the rider must use his legs and back-aids to push the horse's head up by lowering the haunches and bringing his hind-legs more under him and *not* attempt to try and pull it up with the hands.

The rider must "push" the horse's head up.

There are two ways in which to supple a horse :—

1. *From front to back.* This can be done by continually changing the pace, *i.e.*, trot-walk-trot-halt-trot, etc. In this manner if, when reducing the pace, the horse is made to lower his haunches thus driving the hind-legs under him, it produces an exercise which has the effect of suppling the spine. But if he is allowed to reduce pace or to stop on his forehand with a resisting jaw, the exercise is useless as it would only confirm the horse in a bad habit.

2. *Laterally.* For this the rider must at first perform large circles in one direction and then in the other, always being careful during the transition from one rein to the other that the horse does not throw up his head, shorten his stride or offer any resistance. He can then gradually

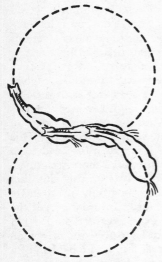

Suppling the horse's spine by performing circles.

reduce the size of the circles until the horse will perform a small circle of 7 metres diameter and change direction without changing his rhythm or raising his head. But this size of circle must not be attempted until he is supple, obedient and remains on the bit. It is most important that, during the transition from one circle to the other, the horse must change his bend from one side to the other without showing any resistance whatever. This exercise supples the spine laterally, as does the shoulder-in (see p. 116).

It is best to make corrections at a trot; the better the move-

The horse must change the bend as he changes direction.

ment the better the response. At the walk the horse would lose forward impulsion and at the canter he is more inclined to stiffen and become stilted. This is not to say no corrections can be made at these paces, but the horse should be made to understand the asking aid and respond to it first at the trot. If, at the canter, he continues to resist and does not respond to this aid, the rider should come back to a trot and perform more suppling exercises before attempting the canter again.

It is very wrong to use the asking aid to both sides; in other words a see-saw movement with the reins. This would have the effect of making the horse turn his head from side to side and it would also make him take more weight on the rein on the stiff side (see p. 104) as it is on this side that he likes to take a stronger hold; also he would most likely become overbent and shorten his stride. In order to get the horse to relax his jaw and take an even pressure on BOTH sides of his mouth, the asking aid must be to the side on which he resists, and the rein on the soft side must be held lightly and still in order to get the effect of the asking rein. The legs must be used at the same time, the one on the side of the asking rein the stronger.

If the horse resists to the right it means his muscles on that side are longer than those on the left because he is naturally bent slightly to the left. The object of the asking rein is to make him straight by lengthening and suppling the muscles on the soft and hollow side. The aids are reversed should the horse be stiff on the left.

The Half-Halt

This is the most important aid in training; it is, in fact, the asking aid, and its objects are:—

1. To ask for a relaxation of the jaw and make the horse straight.

2. To supple him longitudinally.

3. To call the horse's attention to any alteration of pace or direction.

The use of this squeezing-water-out-of-a-sponge aid on the resisting side of a horse's mouth together with the use of the back and both legs, the one on the asking side the stronger, demands a relaxation of the jaw and, at the same time, makes the horse straight by causing him to bend slightly to the stiff side, thus lengthening the muscles on the hollow side which supples him longitudinally. It also makes him take an even pressure on both reins which is the ultimate aim of all trainers.

A horse will nearly always change his rhythm when turning a corner or altering pace. If this aid is used *before* any different movement is requested, the rider, in effect, tells his horse: "take care, I am going to do something different"; and the horse will immediately pay attention and perform the movement without any alteration of balance or rhythm.

Balance and Collection

Because of his long neck and head and the fact of having a rider on his back which in itself upsets his balance, the horse has a natural preponderance of weight on his forehand. To counter-balance this he must be taught to bring more weight on to his hindquarters. This can be achieved by the rider performing half-halts by using his seat and leg aids together with light hands (see p. 110). Never give more leg aid than can be stopped with the hands and never more hand-aid than can be controlled with the legs. In this way the horse is taught to take more weight on his hindquarters by bending his hocks more, thus bringing them further under his body by lowering the quarters. This lightens the forehand and improves the balance of the horse.

Collection can only be obtained after the horse has learnt to hold the bit lightly in his mouth, taking an even pressure on both reins; in other words, when he is in balance. Only then, and this is important, can the rider try to get any collection. It is obtained in the same way by the rider performing half-halts, always with a light contact. Should the horse take too strong a hold at any time the exercise must be stopped immediately and the horse made soft again by the hand on the stiff side making a series of motions like squeezing-water-out-of-a-sponge while keeping a steady contact with the other rein before attempting to perform the exercise again. It must be stressed that, while the hand on the stiff side is acting, the leg on the same side must act at the girth and the other hand on the soft side must hold the rein still with a light contact whilst the leg on this side must act behind the girth to stop the horse from throwing out his hind-legs and thus evading the rider's demands. In this way the horse learns to hold the bit, taking the same contact on both sides of his mouth. All these exercises should be done at the trot. It is better to perform suppling exercises on a large circle as the horse can find his balance easier than on a straight line.

It is not only easier for a horse to work on a large circle than on a straight line, but it is also easier for the rider to make corrections. To ride a circle correctly the horse's spine should comply with the direction of the movement and follow the circumference of the circle. The hind feet should follow exactly the tracks made by the fore feet. They may be in or over them, but never to one side or the other except in lateral work. The horse should not be asked to perform a small circle until he is supple and remains on the bit. The smaller the circle, the more active must be the hind legs in order that they may bend enough to follow the tracks made by the fore feet.

The horse must always look to the way he is going (except in the shoulder-in, p. 116). In performing a right circle he must be bent in a curve round the rider's right leg (see p. 109). He must accept the bit lightly. Incorrect exercises should be repeated until correct, then the horse should be rewarded by being allowed to relax by walking on a long rein. But this must be active; he should not be allowed to slop along.

The Canter

The horse should be made to break off into a canter first on a large circle, gradually straightening it out until he can strike off on either leg on a straight line. The rider must take care to see that the horse does not swing his quarters to one side. When breaking into a canter his body must remain straight, with the hind feet following exactly the tracks made by the fore feet.

The aids to the canter have previously been described on p. 42, but it is as well to reflect on this. The canter aid is a very easy one for the horse to learn and, if it becomes sloppy by the rider just bringing his outside leg back and forgetting to use the inside one, he can get into great difficulties later when he wants to go further with the horse's training and teach him lateral work. This aid is very like the aid for the half-pass, so it is important for the rider to be very exact and to make sure that the outside leg is passive. Its only function is to keep the hind legs from going outwards. It is the INSIDE leg which is the important one, together with the seat and back aids, to direct the horse into a canter. In this way he will not be confused when later taught the half-pass.

He must be taught to go from a canter back to a trot, when the first step must be a correct trot-step and not a shuffle forward for a stride or two. If the rider sits heavy in the saddle by using strong back and leg aids and at the same time asks with the rein on the resisting side, the horse will soon learn to come back to the trot without losing balance or rhythm. A canter straight into a walk and finally into a halt is more difficult. This must only be attempted when the rider is quite sure his horse will answer his seat aids and relax his back muscles by lowering his quarters and producing more active hock action. If the horse is stiff in the back he will not be able to go correctly from a canter into a walk. He would either just fall on his shoulder and become heavy on the hands, or show resistance by throwing up his head and coming off the bit with a hollow back. It is important that all these exercises should be progressive, and one movement must be perfect and performed smoothly before the next one is attempted. Also, they must be performed with lowered haunches and hind-legs well under the horse, otherwise he will get all his weight on his forehand which would mean the rider going back to the beginning and starting all over again. No movement must be carried out with the horse's weight on his forehand except the turn on the forehand. The trainer must be very strict about this. Whenever the horse attempts to throw his weight forward the movement must be stopped immediately and suppling exercises recommenced until he is once more balanced and sitting on his hocks.

It is difficult to supple a horse at the canter because he will only become heavy in the hand when he tires.

TURN ON THE FOREHAND

It is important to gain control of the haunches so that, on the slightest indication of the rider, the horse will either move or immobilize his hindquarters. To do this the turn on the forehand is an excellent exercise.

The horse is placed alongside, but not too close to, a fence or wall. He must be standing squarely on all four legs. To turn to the right on the forehand the rider turns the horse's head slightly to the right—only enough just to make his right eye visible—and, with the right leg drawn back behind the girths, he pushes the horse's quarters round to the left. The left leg remaining at the girths keeps him from stepping backwards. In this case the off-fore is the pivoting leg which can either pivot or be picked up and put down again in the same place. The horse's off-hind leg should cross over in front of the near-hind. He must not step backwards, but it is a worse fault to step forwards as it means that he has lost his balance. The head must remain still during the whole turn.

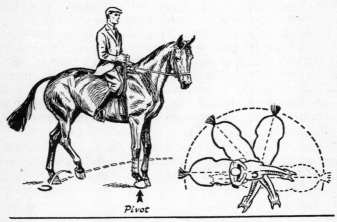

Pivot

The right turn on the forehand.

To turn to the left on the forehand the aids are reversed. This exercise when once learnt need not be performed again, as it is merely a means of knowing whether the rider has control of the horse's haunches or not. Until he has this he must not try to perform any more advanced exercises.

THE COUNTER-CANTER

This is also an excellent suppling exercise, but it must not be attempted too early; until the horse is supple he cannot perform it correctly. He will start changing legs behind and this is a very difficult habit to cure.

First try long and not very deep serpentines at the canter. For instance, canter in a school or alongside a fence on the right leg; then bring the horse off the track and return to the track without changing legs. The rider must remember to keep the horse slightly bent to the right, even when going to the left, as it is important for him to keep the bend towards the leading leg. As the horse gets more supple these serpentines can get deeper and deeper, until the rider can take his horse round a school in a counter-canter and finally perform a complete circle. (This means going round to the left with the right leg leading, or vice versa.) Progress must be gradual and the rider must be content with a little at a time. It is far better to go slowly and get it right, than to hurry in the early stages and then later have to correct other faults which have been produced by 'forcing the pace'. Naturally the exercises must be practised equally on both reins.

The counter-canter must not be confused with the disunited canter, which is an evasion and is always incorrect. In the true canter one pair of laterals (both legs on one side) should be in advance of the other pair (see p. 40). In the disunited canter the horse is leading with the near-fore and off-hind, or vice versa.

The Shoulder-in

This is an excellent suppling exercise. When performed correctly it makes the horse bend slightly at the ribs whilst it activates the inside hock. If incorrect it can do a lot of damage. A horse can produce a lot of evasions in this exercise. He can bend his neck only and so evade the effort to bend at the ribs, while he remains going on one track with the hind legs following the same direction as the fore legs. In this way all he acquires is a rubber neck which makes evasions in other movements easy for him. He can also throw out his hind legs instead of bringing the forehand in thus avoiding having to bend the inside hock; thus the exercise is useless.

For a right shoulder-in the forehand should be brought off the track as if about to start a circle, but, instead of continuing the circle the rider's inside (right) leg, held at the girth, pushes the horse's forehand to the left so that the

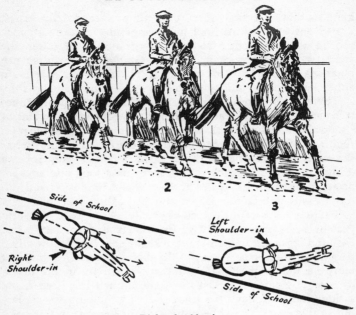

Right shoulder-in

horse will continue going forward with the head, neck and spine, following a curve of which the centre is the rider's right leg. At the same time the rider keeps the horse's hind legs on the track and his quarters from going to the left by bringing his left leg back behind the girth thus controlling the quarters and maintaining the impulsion (see above).

The easiest way to start a shoulder-in is on a bend. The rider comes round the corner applying the above aids and, instead of straightening out after the corner, he holds this position. If the horse responds by performing just two steps sideways the pressure of the inside leg should be relaxed immediately and the horse allowed to go forward into a large half circle. It is better to continue on a circle than to bring the forehand back to the track, because the horse, being already bent in that direction, should be allowed to do the easiest movement as a reward for having responded to the aid. He can be asked to return to the straight line again after the shoulder-in as his work improves. Gradually the horse can be asked to do more steps until he will perform this exercise to either hand for quite long stretches.

This exercise should be performed at the trot, but sometimes it is easier at first to teach the horse to understand the aids at the walk. However, as soon as he understands what is required of him the trot should be employed. The better the movement the better the exercise and it is dangerous to do too much work at the walk, except on a long rein as a relaxation, as at this pace the horse will lose impulsion and can more easily produce evasions and get behind the bit.

There are different degrees of shoulder-in. It is better to get the horse moving on two different tracks so that, while the hind legs continue on one track, the fore legs follow a line parallel to them (see p. 117). In this way the rider will get more flexibility of the spine and more activity in the inside hind leg. Some riders ask for only a small bend when the inside hind leg follows the track made by the outside fore leg, but in this case he must be quite sure the horse is in this position and not just bending his neck. Force must not be used or attempted if the horse throws up his head or puts up an evasion. The head and neck must remain still and in the correct position. To perform the left shoulder-in, the aids are reversed.

In order to appreciate the importance of the shoulder-in as a suppling exercise it must be realised that it is another way of making the horse straight by making him bend on his stiff side thus lengthening the muscles on the hollow side; it also activates his inner hind leg which makes him more supple.

The Extended Trot

This must on no account be attempted until the horse has learnt collection, otherwise he will do one of two things:—

1. Run, which means he is quickening his pace instead
   of lengthening it.
2. The extensions will come from in front with the hind
   legs trailing. Both are incorrect.

From the collected trot the horse should be asked to lengthen
his stride by a strong use of the leg, back and seat aids. Only
a few paces should be asked at first, and if the rhythm is lost he
must be stopped quietly and the exercise repeated. It is best
to start on a large circle by asking for a few lengthened steps,
bringing him back to collection and asking him to lengthen
again. When this is achieved some long strides can be asked on a
straight line. The rider must not expect too much extension
to commence with, only seeking an even pace. Gradually,
as the horse understands, more extension can be demanded
When correct he may be rewarded by a lively walk on a long
rein. The horse must lengthen his stride when asked with
the motive power coming from behind. The hands must allow
him to stretch his neck but the weight on the reins must not
be increased.

Simple Change of Leg

When the horse can perform a canter-walk correctly he is
then ready for a simple change of leg. It is necessary
before starting this exercise to be sure the horse will strike
off into a canter on either leg on a straight line and remain
perfectly straight when doing so. It would be a mistake to
try a simple change of leg if the horse throws his quarters in
when striking off into a canter as it would only aggravate this
fault; then there would be many difficulties to overcome in
order to get a correct change of leg. The reason for correct
canter-aids is now obvious. If the rider's inside leg and
seat are used to direct the horse into a canter while the outside
leg behind the girth is passive he will not learn this annoying
habit of pushing his quarters to the inside when striking off
into a canter and there would be no need for any corrections
when commencing the simple change.

To practise this movement the rider canters off on a named leg, performs a canter-to-walk and walks on for some distance before striking off on the other leg. He then gradually reduces the length of the walk in between the canters until there are only two or three paces at the walk. The resulting simple change of leg will have been performed with the greatest of ease.

This is the correct simple change of leg; but in all tests up to medium class this change can be done progressively through a trot. There must, however, always be a few paces performed at the walk.

PIROUETTE TO THE RIGHT

To perform a half pirouette to the right at the walk the rider should ask for a half-halt and, only if there is no resistance from the horse, bring his forehand off the track with both hands, the right leg at girth to maintain impulsion and keep the horse from stepping backwards, the left leg behind the girth to prevent him from swinging his quarters to the left, gradually bringing the forehand round the quarters (see opposite). The horse must not step back so only two steps should be attempted at a time when he must be sent forwards. Only when the horse puts up no resistance can more steps be tried and so on until the entire half pirouette is accomplished. To commence with it is better to perform a small concentric circle with the hind legs which should be reduced gradually until the horse, as he turns, is marking time with his inner hind leg.

The rider must be careful to see that the horse does not pivot with his inside hind leg. It is important that he keeps up the walk stride all the time. Force should not be used. Directly the horse puts up an evasion or becomes heavy on the hand, the exercise must cease and the horse must be taken back on to the circle and made soft before proceeding with further steps of the pirouette. For a left pirouette the aids are reversed.

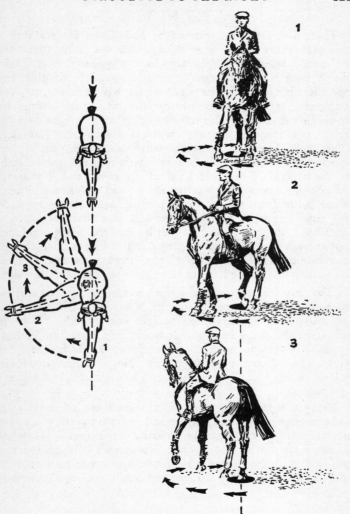

Pirouette to the right

THE RIDER

Hard and fast rules cannot be laid down for training a horse as every horse is different. All the same there are basic rules which should be kept in mind. Some horses take much longer than others, so it is impossible to give any specific time. But if the work so far has been correct, the horse should be permanently on the bit, which means he is holding it lightly in his mouth taking equal weight on both reins and obeying the aids without resistance. Naturally there will always be moments when the horse puts up an evasion and resists the bit, but he should respond immediately to a correction given. If he does not obey, and if there is no obvious reason, like excitement caused by another horse, a car going down the road or a bird suddenly flying up, then the rider must ask himself why, and what has been wrong with his training. It may be that he uses too much hand and not enough leg. It maybe that he is stiff himself, which will communicate itself at once to the horse with dire results. Or it may be that he has not been clear enough with his aids.

It is very important for the rider to analyse himself and be sure he is sitting correctly. If he is getting too far forward he will not be in a position to give correct aids. If he is sitting in the shape of a bow it would be impossible for him to use his back to push the horse forward. If he loses his temper he will never get anywhere. So, if things go wrong, the rider must not blame the horse but himself and correct his position.

Every day the rider must go over all these exercises and, as time goes on, he can ask for and insist on getting a better performance always aiming towards perfection. He must be more strict with not-so-good movements. If the rider is satisfied with the progress his horse has made, he may now take his training a step further and teach him the half-pass.

THE HALF-PASS

The left half-pass.

The horse is now supple, his rhythm established, his head is steady and he accepts the bit and will answer leg aids, so the half-pass can be commenced. A horse normally moves on one track, that is, the tracks made by the hind feet following exactly those made by the fore feet. When the horse is asked to move sideways the tracks made by the hind feet are separate from those made by the fore feet and he moves forwards and to one side or the other on two tracks. The easiest way to start a left half-pass, pictured above, is when the rider comes round the corner on the short side of the school and is entering the long side on the left turn. The horse is now bent in the correct position for a left half-pass. The rider brings his right leg back behind the girths, which holds the horse's quarters preventing them from following the tracks made by the fore feet. The left leg at the girths keeps up the impulsion and the horse, finding he cannot allow his quarters to follow his forehand, goes on two tracks. For a right half-pass the aids are reversed.

An alternative way of starting the half-pass is to perform a half circle and bring the horse back to the side of the school on two tracks in the same way, using the same aids.

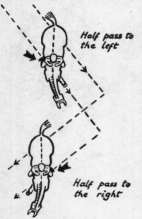

Half pass to the left

Half pass to the right

The rider must be careful not to attempt to start this movement while the horse shows any resistance as he would only increase the resistance when asked to perform this rather difficult exercise. He should sit slightly to the left (see p. 123); the left rein holds the position and shows the direction, with the right rein supporting. The horse should be slightly looking in the direction to which he is going with his body parallel to the side of the arena. He must maintain his rhythm and free forward movement and not shorten his stride.

The legs on the side to which the horse is moving are known as the inside legs, whilst those on the other side are called the outside legs. The horse's outside legs should cross in front of the inside legs and should move well forward. The rider's outside leg only holds the quarters, it does not push; if this happens the rider will lose his balance by collapsing the outside hip and throwing his weight to the outside, which would have the effect of making the horse turn his head away from the movement and get more into a position of a right shoulder-in. The rider's inside leg must act because, as it drives the horse forward and he finds his hind legs are controlled by the rider's outside leg, he moves sideways as well.

Mostly a horse will evade by throwing his weight on his inside shoulder and turning his head the opposite way. When this happens he must be stopped immediately, suppled up again and, when light and showing no resistance, the movement can be repeated. Only a few steps should be asked and, when performed, the horse patted and rewarded by a walk on a long rein.

THE REIN-BACK

1   2

It is not good to ask a horse to rein-back too often as it may encourage him to get behind the bit and, when asked to stand still, he might start anticipating the rein-back. Although it is important for him to know how to rein-back, it is for this reason this movement has been placed last and, when once learned, it should only be practised occasionally.

The rider brings his horse to a halt by closing both legs and sitting heavy by using his back aids. At the same time he asks with the rein on the stiff side, resisting slightly with the other. This action is kept up after the horse has come to a halt and, finding he cannot go forward, he steps backward. The pace is in 2-time. The horse must not break his diagonals when stepping back, thus turning it into a 4-time movement. He must rein-back by lifting each diagonal pair at the same time.

He must not be pulled back

He must not be pulled back or else he will throw up his head and hollow his back and then he could not step backward correctly. He must keep his head still and step back perfectly straight (see 1 and 2, p. 125).

DIFFICULT HORSES

If a horse has been correctly schooled he should not get into bad habits, but if no such care has been taken of him when young he may develop any of the following vices :—

A rearer.

Rearing

This is a very unpleasant habit as the horse may lose his balance and fall over backwards hurting probably both himself and his rider. It is very difficult, if not impossible, to cure. Lots of different methods have been tried without real success and the only thing the rider can do is to throw the reins to the horse, get well forward, even to clasping him round the neck and use all his power to try to get the horse to go forward. It is a very bad habit and very difficult to deal with.

A horse out of control.

A Puller

Should a rider find himself in the unfortunate position of being run away with, it will be useless for him to take a steady pull on the horse's mouth as this would only deaden the feeling in the mouth and would cause him to pull harder. He could try and reduce the pace by taking a strong hold of the rein on the soft side, and giving and taking with the other rein. Should he take a firm hold on the stiff side as well, it would only have the effect of making the horse take a still stronger hold—should this fail, he could try a sawing movement with the reins, but this would be detrimental to the horse's mouth. If he is in an open field the rider could pull the horse's head round in one direction and continue going round in a circle until the horse stops. The last two courses would be very detrimental to the horse's mouth and should only be attempted in the case of an emergency.

This horse will need very skilful handling. He should be put back in a snaffle bridle and school work started again right from the beginning. The rider should *never* allow him *to lean on the bit,* but gradually he must be taught by a series of half-halts to carry himself at all paces with only a light weight on the rider's hands. It is a long and tedious school, but one well worth while with a good horse. Certainly the more the rider pulls, the more the horse will too, and, as he is much the stronger, he will always win.

For hunting when the owner has no time in which to school his horse, another bit might be found to suit him, but a softer one rather than a stronger one is more likely to succeed, *i.e.,* a snaffle or gag-snaffle with a standing martingale would be much better than a large curb bit or anything with a curb-chain which has a nutcracker action.

A puller is practically always the result of a bit injury or a rough handed rider, therefore, his mouth should be made as comfortable as possible with a bit that does not hurt him and when he gets his confidence he will soon cease to fight against it.

Keep a kicker away from other horses.

Kicker

This horse is a nuisance and the rider must be very careful to keep him away from people and other horses. This is especially so out hunting when a lot of people congregate together in a gate-way. The owner of this horse must keep behind and wait till last before he goes through the gate. He must also be very careful to keep away from hounds. **There is no known cure.**

Teach your horse to stand still while mounting.

A difficult horse to mount

This is a matter of patience. The horse must first be held by one or two people if necessary. He should be put in the corner of a yard or school. The rider must then put one foot in the stirrup and take it out again, repeating this several times. Directly the horse stands still while he does this he can go one step further and take his weight on the stirrup and then get down again. This performance must be carried out again and again going one step further each time the horse stands still. In the end it will be found that the horse does not move until the rider is in the saddle and gives him the aid to go on. It should be the first lesson to teach a horse and it is one he learns very easily.

Nervous and excitable horses

This sort of horse must be treated with great patience and care. Never hurry him at his work, never punish him for wrong-doing, only be firm and repeat the exercise until he realises what is required of him and that there is nothing to fear. Take him up to strange objects allowing him to look

Take your horse up to strange objects.

at them before making him pass them. Coax him rather than force him and, when the rider has got his complete confidence, he will find that the horse soon forgets his nervousness and will become a willing and gentle companion.

An excitable horse must be worked very quietly. The rider must try and make the horse trot slowly with a long rein and a light contact. This would be easiest on a large circle—should the horse increase his pace he must be brought back by a series of half-halts until he keeps the same pace. It would be useless to work him hard for many hours. This would only have the effect of making him tired and would not relax the tension. Sometimes he will settle with good hard hunting, but riders who are not experienced are advised to avoid these horses.

Napping

A nappy horse is one that tries to assert its will against that of the rider. It may show itself in several forms such as refusing to leave home, trying to go in a different direction to which the rider wishes, refusing to jump and so on. He is a most difficult horse to deal with.

If a young horse starts to nap the great thing is to win the first battle even if it means standing in the same place for an hour or even more, but the rider must persevere no matter how long it takes him. He must never get off his horse and lead him, unless there is any question of danger to himself or the horse, as that counts as a victory in the mind of the horse.

If the rider is sure that the horse is not frightened but is just self-willed, this is one occasion when the stick may be used to advantage but again it must be stressed that it is no use using the stick unless the rider is sure of winning the battle and making the horse do as he is told.

It is most important to establish in the mind of the horse that the rider is master, if he once realises this is not the case he will always try to disobey and want his own way. If a horse is confirmed in this habit it is as well to leave him to the experts to deal with.

CONCLUSION

It should be remembered that riding is just as much an art as music or painting. In order to gain even a modicum of success in training a horse, the rider will find that he must not only discipline his horse, but himself as well. Like every athlete he must bring his muscles up to the finest possible pitch so that he becomes supple and strong. He should practise riding without stirrups, and, if he can get somebody to help him, he will derive tremendous benefit from being lunged. The more he can do this, the stronger will his seat become so that he will never have to resort to the reins in order to remain in the saddle. When he has achieved this he will find he can give the most delicate aids to the horse as his hands, relieved of all effort to keep his balance, will become soft and sensitive, and his seat, being strong and independent, will enable him to give accurate leg and back-aids.

Each horse he rides will produce a different problem and he must learn to understand each one and be able to "tune-in" to the most difficult and intractable horse. But all this takes a long time, many years of study and riding many different horses, making many mistakes and having many failures.

In training a horse the rider should make out a programme as it is most important to work progressively. He should be taken step by step carefully through all the exercises. It is a great mistake to hurry a horse during his training and to start a new exercise before he understands the previous one. In this way the horse will get muddled and then he either gets excited and hots up or he loses his rhythm and his movements become restricted.

The rider will find it is better to do all schooling work in an ordinary snaffle bridle because it is a mild bit and is the least likely to hurt the horse's mouth. It is the easiest bridle in which to teach the horse to relax, to lower his head and to accept the bit. All horses should be able to perform all their work in a snaffle right up to the high school movements of piaffe and passage. It will then be found that they will take immediately to a double bridle without any fuss or worry. If a double bridle is used too soon it will be inclined to make the horse take a stronger hold and set his jaw. This would have the effect of putting more weight on the forehand, so defeating the rider's object, which is to get the weight back on hindquarters thus lightening the forehand and making the horse step more under the body with his hind legs. Or it may make him open his mouth and get behind the bit when he will lose his impulsion and not go freely forward.

The rider can test if his work is correct by a simple method. If it is correct, when he "gives" the reins the horse should lower and stretch his neck. If the teaching is wrong, when the reins are loose the horse will throw up his head for relaxation which means that the rider is trying to force the horse into a certain position which invariably creates stiffness.

The amount of work a horse needs varies with the temperament of the animal. Generally speaking, a horse should

be worked hard for 45 minutes to 1 hour a day. But during this
time his attention must be kept on his work and he should not
be allowed to idle, even during moments of relaxation, when
he must be made to walk on. He can then be taken for a
walk to cool off. The rider will find at first that he becomes
hot while the horse keeps cool, then both the horse and his rider
get hot, finally it should be the horse who sweats and the rider
who remains cool because the horse should now be working
with less effort on the part of his trainer. It is an excellent
sign if the horse sweats between his hind-legs as it means
he is really driving from behind and using his back muscles.

After the horse becomes more advanced in his work, or if
he is very young and weak, the rider may find that 30 minutes
schooling is enough; he can then be taken out for a hack or
given a jump in order to keep him interested. The art is to
do neither too much work nor too little. The trainer must
find this out for himself but on the whole 45 minutes to 1
hour per day is long enough to keep a horse's interest, make
him fit and gradually build up strong and supple muscles.
To continue work when the horse is tired is only to defeat its
own object.

When training a horse it is better for nobody else to
ride him so that he does not get muddled by slightly different
aids. But there are many business people who can ride only
at week-ends. These people can work their horses as
suggested in this book when they are able to ride, and, during
the week, in order to keep the horse fit it would be sufficient
to get a friend to walk him out on a long loose rein. He can
be ridden along the lanes to get him used to traffic, or across
a farm, but he should be kept at the walk with as little contact
as possible with the mouth. In this way the young horse
will remain calm, will get used to walking about the country
and seeing different sights, and at the same time it will not
interrupt or interfere with his schooling which should be
carried out by one person. During the summer months
the owner may find it possible to give his horse enough
work either in the early morning or late in the evening. In

this case it would not be necessary for the horse to have further exercise.

In conclusion the advanced horse should give himself freely and willingly and should seek out the wishes of his rider so that he can perform whatever movement he is asked with fluidity and grace.   Finally, it is well to remember that "the gods confer their blessing only at the price of labour" and both horse and rider must, therefore, submit to the discipline of endless repetition.   Only in this way will perfection be obtained.

———————————

STARTING TENNIS

C. M. Jones and Angela Buxton

An exciting, illustrated guide, *Starting Tennis* offers beginners innovative instruction at the most crucial time — as they begin to establish their tennis skills.

Written from the combined experience of two internationally known coaches, C. M. Jones and Angela Buxton, *Starting Tennis* gives a remarkable summary of everything the aspiring player will need to know. Apart from chapters on how the game is played, on stroke-making, serving, elementary tactical play and practice programs, the book contains essential information on coaching, tennis clubs, tournaments, and an enormous number of valuable hints and tips for both on and off the court. It provides the key to rapid progress in the game which all beginning players hope to find.

As essential as a racket, *Starting Tennis* is required reading for all beginning players, particularly young beginners. $5.95 paper